SERBIA AND MONTENEGRO

David C. King

BENCHMARK BOOKS

MARSHALL CAVENDISH
NEW YORK

PICTURE CREDITS
Cover: © George Spenceley/Art Directors
AFP: 25, 27, 31, 33, 35, 36, 37, 38, 41, 43, 54, 56, 60, 62, 64, 81, 86, 98, 99, 101, 102, 108, 114, 118 • alt.TYPE /REUTERS: 80 • Giulio Andreini: 5, 20, 32, 48, 70, 78, 79, 89, 91, 97, 103, 105, 115, 117, 119 • COPIX/Laurence Mitchell: 61, 107 • Corbis Inc.: 13, 14, 85, 113, 121 • T.E. Clark/Eye Ubiquitous: 106 • Melanie Friend/Eye Ubiquitous: 42, 67, 68, 84 • Jeremy Horner/Eye Ubiquitous: 29, 34, 52, 58, 129 • Peter Moszynski/Eye Ubiquitous: 6, 11, 40 • Nigel Sitwell/Eye Ubiquitous: 104 • Focus Team Italy: 4, 10, 19, 44, 76, 122 • Haga Library, Inc.: 63 • HBL Network Photo Agency: 77, 83 • Karl Hughes: 53 • Lonely Planet Images: 1, 3, 8, 15, 16, 21, 49, 51, 59, 66, 71, 73, 87, 92, 96, 100, 109, 111, 116, 123, 124, 126, 127, 130 • MC Picture Library (Chef Wan Around the World): 125 • Museum of Vuk and Dositej: 88 • Lister Louise/Stockfood: 131 • TopFoto: 7, 12, 17, 18, 22, 23, 24, 26, 28, 30, 45, 46, 47, 55, 65, 72, 74, 82, 93, 95, 110, 112 • Travel Ink Ltd: 9, 39, 50, 69, 94, 128 • www.kosovo.com: 120

ACKNOWLEDGMENTS
Thanks to Gordon N. Bardos, Assistant Director, Harriman Institute, Columbia University, for his expert reading of this manuscript.

PRECEDING PAGE
A family in Kosovo sets up a stall in a bazaar that was damaged by a bombing raid during the recent civil war.

Marshall Cavendish Benchmark
99 White Plains Road
Tarrytown, NY 10591
Website: www.marshallcavendish.us

© Marshall Cavendish International (Asia) Private Limited 2005
® "Cultures of the World" is a registered trademark of Marshall Cavendish Corporation.

Series concept and design by Times Editions
An imprint of Marshall Cavendish International (Asia) Private Limited,
A member of Times Publishing Limited

Library of Congress Cataloging-in-Publication Data
King, David C.
   Serbia and Montenegro / by David C. King.
      p. cm. — (Cultures of the world)
   Includes bibliographical references and index.
   ISBN 0-7614-1855-5
   1. Serbia and Montenegro—Juvenile literature. I. Title. II. Series.
DR1940.K56 2004
949.71—dc22   2004022248

Printed in China

7 6 5 4 3 2

CONTENTS

Sveti Stefan, a fishing village turned into a top class resort hotel, is one of Montenegro's biggest tourist attractions.

St. Peter's monastery in Cetinje, Montenegro.

INTRODUCTION

TO MOST OUTSIDERS, the Balkan peninsula in southeastern Europe is a perplexing jigsaw puzzle, made up of different ethnic, religious, and geographic pieces—with Yugoslavia in the middle. In the 1990s, Yugoslavia was torn apart by civil war. Four of the six Yugoslav republics withdrew from the federation: Croatia, Slovenia, Bosnia and Herzegovina, and Macedonia. This left the Federal Republic of Yugoslavia, which now consisted of just two republics, Serbia and Montenegro, plus two autonomous provinces, Kosovo and Vojvodina. In February 2002, the official name of the country was changed to Serbia and Montenegro.

This strife-torn land is located at one of the world's great crossroads, where the peoples and cultures of Europe and western Asia have met for more than 2,000 years. It is a region that has witnessed a great mixing of empires, religions, and ethnic groups. Sorting out the pieces of this puzzle to understand the present is not easy, but it is well worth the effort.

GEOGRAPHY

SERBIA AND MONTENEGRO IS A LAND of rugged beauty; nearly half the land is hilly or mountainous. Visitors are awed by the steep canyons carved through imposing mountains, and by the clear, swift streams at the bottom of narrow gorges. In other places, the beauty is more serene—coastal fishing villages on the Adriatic Sea and peaceful farm villages in the river valleys.

The geography of Serbia and Montenegro can be divided into three regions: the Pannonian Plain, which is an extension of the Great Plain of Hungary (where Magyar cowboys on horseback once herded cattle); the coastal region, which is entirely within Montenegro; and the interior highlands, forming the most rugged part of the country.

Above: **This valley is found near Bar, a town along the southern coast of Montenegro.**

Opposite: **An old town, located on a small peninsula, faces the Budva Bay on the Adriatic Sea.**

THE PANNONIAN PLAIN

In the northern region, the interior highlands flatten out to form the Pannonian plain, a region of grassland similar to the great plains of North America. The area was once covered by the Pannonian Sea. Over thousands of years, alluvial deposits from the mountains gradually filled in the sea, leaving rich layers of soil, which make this ideal agricultural land.

The plain extends along the Danube River and its tributaries, including the Sava, Tisa, and Drava. The danger of floods has been reduced by building dikes and canals. More than half of Serbia and Montenegro's farms are located in these fertile lowlands.

The climate here is more extreme than in the other two regions. Summer temperatures often soar above 100°F (37.7°C), and during the long, cold winter the temperature may fall below -10°F (-23.3°C).

THE COASTAL REGION

The coastal region is a narrow, rocky strip of land that hugs the shoreline of the Adriatic Sea. At sea level on the Gulf of Kotor, greenery provides a lush contrast against the gray backdrop of the Dinaric Alps, which rise steeply behind the shore. The white sand beaches of resort towns draw tourists from all parts of Europe. Many of the fishing villages have long histories, like the town of Budva, one of the oldest on the Adriatic. Over the centuries Budva has been home to ancient Phoenicians, Illyrians, Greeks, and Romans, and later Venetians, Austrians, and Serbs.

The coast enjoys a Mediterranean climate of dry, sun-filled summers, with temperatures averaging 75°F (24°C) in July. Winters are rainy and cool. January temperatures average 45°F (7°C), but rarely fall below freezing.

An old fortification, which may date as far back as the 16th century, overlooks Budva Bay.

A few miles inland, the land features limestone outcroppings called karst terrain. This is a landscape in which water and carbon dioxide (from the air) form a mild acid that slowly erodes soft areas of limestone. This creates deep holes called chimneys, as well as long depressions and underground caves that carve honeycomb-like webs below the surface, often extending over several miles.

THE INTERIOR HIGHLANDS

The jagged peaks and broad ridges of the Dinaric Alps run parallel to the coast and dominate the western part of Serbia and Montenegro, while the Balkan mountains form the eastern border. In some places the steep cliffs of the Dinarics reach to the coast. Some of the narrow canyons offer breathtaking views of the rivers sparkling far below, such as the canyon of the Tara River—one of the longest and deepest in the world.

Although parts of the Dinarics and the Balkans display spectacular scenery, large areas seem bleak and desolate. In winter cold winds called the bora roar down from the north. The winds do not bring much snow, but the cold is bitter and unrelenting. Journalist Milovan Djilas wrote, "All living things, and all the works of mankind, can be lost on these stony heights; [and] sound crumbles to nothing on the sharp contours of the cliffs."

Throughout history foreign invaders have found it difficult to control large areas because small bands could take cover in mountain strongholds. For more than 500 years the Ottoman Turks ruled much of the Balkan lands, but they could never completely subdue Montenegro.

Children play on snow-covered hills in Kosovo.

Zabljak, the highest town in the Balkans at 4,777 feet (1,456 m) above sea level, is located in Durmitor National Park in Montenegro.

Although only a few miles from the Adriatic, the climate of the highlands is very different from the coast. Generally the region has a moderate continental climate, but there can be extremes in both summer and winter. January temperatures average 32°F (0°C), for example, but there can be long stretches with the thermometer below 14°F (-10°C); summer temperatures average 68 to 72°F (20 to 22°C), but can reach 86°F (30°C) for several days.

The highlands are on an unstable section of tectonic plates, making earthquakes a constant danger. A serious earthquake in 1979 killed several hundred people and destroyed entire towns.

LAKE SCUTARI

Located on the border between Montenegro and Albania, Lake Scutari (*right*) is the largest on the Balkan Peninsula.

Once an arm of the Adriatic Sea, the lake is now separated from the sea by a narrow strip of land. Steep mountains rise dramatically above the water on the west and northwest. Six rivers flow into Scutari, and a seventh—the Bojana River—flows out the southern end and drains into the Adriatic.

Small picturesque villages dot the shoreline around the lake. Several are well-known for their old monasteries and fortresses, some dating back to the 13th century.

RIVERS AND LAKES

In Montenegro, clear, fast-moving rivers flow through steep-sided canyons into the Adriatic Sea. In the rest of the country, the rivers flow northward and northeastward into the Danube and the Danube into the Black Sea.

The Danube, one of Europe's great rivers, runs through Serbia and Montenegro for about 225 miles (362 km) and forms part of the border with Romania for another 142 miles (228.5 km). Together with its tributaries, the system drains nearly 70 percent of the total land area.

There are more than a hundred natural lakes in the two republics. Some are in depressions left by the glaciers of the last Ice Age (which receded about 12,000 years ago). People call these glacial lakes the eyes of the mountains because of the clear blue of the water. Other lakes fill hollows near the coast of the Adriatic Sea, including the largest in the region—Lake Scutari (Skadarsko Jezero in Serbo-Croatian)—which straddles the border with Albania.

SERBIA AND MONTENEGRO

After the fall of Communism in 1989–90, four of the republics that made up Yugoslavia declared their independence. This triggered a four-year civil war, and by 1996 only two republics remained in Yugoslavia—Serbia and Montenegro—along with the two provinces controlled by Serbia, Kosovo and Vojvodina.

Serbia is by far the largest portion of the new country, covering 34,116 square miles (88,361 square km). The republic is surrounded by Hungary, Romania, Bulgaria, Macedonia, Albania, Bosnia-Herzegovina, and Croatia. If Montenegro should break away, which it has a constitutional right to do after 2006, Serbia would be completely landlocked.

Montenegro covers only about 14 percent of the total area—5,333 square miles (13,812 square km)—and has a population of only about 648,000 people, compared with more than 10 million in Serbia. The name Montenegro is Italian for black mountain; in Serbo-Croatian, the name is Crna Cora.

The point at which Montenegro, Serbia, and Albania meet is one of the most imposing mountain areas in the Balkans. The highest mountain on the peninsula is located here—Mount Daravica, at 8,712 feet (2,656 m).

A grey heron tries to catch some fish for food in the Iron Gate section of the Danube River.

ANIMALS

This southeastern corner of Europe has drawn hunters, hikers, fishers, and naturalists from many countries. The forested mountain slopes support a rich array of large animals, including brown bear, roe deer, wild boar, and chamois. These species still thrive in spite of having been hunted for several centuries.

Some species, such as wolf and lynx, have declined largely because of farmers' efforts to get rid of wolves with poison. Both species survived by moving deeper into the mountain regions; new environmental laws are also offering protection. Two new species, introduced in the 20th century, are thriving—the raccoon dog, brought from eastern Asia, and the muskrat, from North America.

Game birds have also been plentiful, but populations declined severely in the 1980s and 1990s because of the war and environmental pollution. Common species include quail, pheasant, grouse, and partridge, plus waterfowl such as geese and various species of ducks.

The waterways of Serbia and Montenegro are well-known for the abundance of fish and birds. The wetlands along the Danube and Sava rivers have been one of the largest nesting grounds for birds in all of Europe. Different species have made use of different parts of the ecosystem. Cormorants and pelicans are found in the deeper waters, for example, while waders such as herons and egrets stand in shallow water to wait for their prey, and shorebirds such as ibis and spoonbills use their unique beaks to dig into the wet sand. The thick reeds form small floating islands in the slow-moving channels, providing excellent nesting sites for a variety of songbirds, such as warblers, rakes, little bitterns, and others.

THE IRON GATE

One of the most spectacular stretches of the Danube River is a 2-mile- (3-km-) long gorge (*below*) called the Iron Gate (Gvozdena Vrata in Serbo-Croatian). The gorge is 530 feet (162 m) wide, but in spite of this breadth, shipping was made difficult by a huge rock, called Perigrada, which blocked the channel near the town of Sip. In 1896 the Sip Canal was completed, solving the problem of shipping around the barrier. Then, in 1972 a joint Romanian-Yugoslav development project quadrupled the amount of shipping through the canal while adding a dam and hydroelectric power station.

In the years since completion of the dam, however, the hydroelectric plant and the dam have contributed to the region's environmental woes. The plant's heated wastewater has contributed to the decline in fish populations and altered the river's natural drainage pattern. The reduction of fish, in turn, has lowered bird populations.

The variety of birds and abundance of fish have also drawn birds of prey. The osprey, for example, are great fishers, and white-tailed eagles, harrier hawks, and red-footed falcons dine on fish as well as other small creatures.

Both bird and fish populations have declined sharply because of overfishing and pollution. The Danube and the Black Sea, for example, were once primary sources of caviar. Caviar is the processed eggs of large fish, such as sturgeon. But overfishing has nearly destroyed the sturgeon population. Because a sturgeon can live 100 years and each female lays more than two million eggs, catching just one female sturgeon has a powerful effect on the future sturgeon population.

Other fish, many of them of commercial value, have also declined, including the wels, a huge catfish species that can weigh up to 440 pounds (200 kg)! A number of these species are found only in the Danube system, such as a species of herring that has adapted to freshwater, and the Romanian bullhead perch, which was discovered less than 50 years ago.

PLANTS

The Serbian and Montenegrin region of the Balkans is an ancient land, with many species of plants dating far back in time. Some species of trees, such as the horse chestnut, originated here an estimated 65 million years ago, and then spread to other parts of the world. There are more than 5,000 plant species in Serbia and Montenegro, and many of them are native to the region. In certain parts of the country, the antiquated farm methods used have enabled some areas to support wetlands and meadows that bloom into glorious fields of wildflowers in the spring. More modern farming methods would change most of these areas into cropland.

Forests still cover almost one-third of the land, mostly in the mountain regions. In the eastern part of the country,

Ripe olives hang from an olive tree in a grove along the Adriatic coast.

deciduous forests (trees that lose their leaves) cover most of the Carpathian and Balkan mountains, while mixed deciduous and coniferous (evergreen) forests are found in the lower elevations of the northern Dinaric Alps. In the southern and western Dinarics, most of the forests have been cleared, causing serious erosion.

Along the Adriatic coast, plants accustomed to a Mediterranean climate have adapted well to the long, dry summers. These plants include palm, olive, fig, orange, and lemon trees, as well as pomegranate shrubs.

SETTLEMENT PATTERNS

The geography of the country and the region has influenced where and how people have settled over the centuries. For example, isolated mountain regions have remained thinly settled, with widely scattered

THE LAND OF CAVES

The karst terrain, with its countless underground caves (*right*), is a paradise for spelunkers—people who explore caves, often as a hobby or sport.

The Postojna cave is one of the most famous. Visitors can explore its nearly 14 miles (23 km) of twists and turns on foot or by a cable railway for part of the distance. During World War II, Hitler's troops stored gasoline in part of the cave. Tito's Partisans found the cache, wired it with dynamite, then detonated it from a safe distance, sending fireballs roaring through the cave.

Experts say that only about 10 percent of the caves have been explored. Some caves, filled with water, are really underground rivers. Of the estimated 1,000 underground rivers in the region, the Trebisnjica River is thought to be the longest in the world.

villages and a few towns. Farms tend to remain small in the mountains, while farms, and even farmhouses, on the plains are larger. During the time of the Roman Empire (about 250 B.C. to A.D. 400) some of the coastal areas developed into prosperous city-states. Farther inland, overland trade routes led to some towns becoming important trade centers.

Belgrade, the capital, offers a good example of how location influences the importance of a community. In ancient times Belgrade's fortress—Kalemegdan—occupied a strategic position, dominating the confluence of the Danube and Sava rivers. Every major military power has fought for control of that location, among them Romans, Celts, Huns, Magyars, Byzantines, Slavs, Avars, Bulgars, Turks, and Serbs. Historians say that Belgrade has been destroyed and rebuilt more than forty times.

In the 20th century, especially after World War II (1939–45), the development of modern industry and transportation has led to dramatic changes in settlement patterns. Large numbers of people have migrated from rural areas to cities and towns. By the 1990s about one-third of the people were living in cities of 20,000 or more.

HISTORY

THE HISTORY OF HUMANS in the Balkans goes back some 200,000 years—earlier than in any other part of Europe. However, a clear picture of how people lived does not emerge until the Neolithic Period (New Stone Age) about 7000 B.C. Between 7000 and 3500 B.C. people were living in settled farm villages in the Pannonian Basin, along the Sava and Danube rivers. These societies, which archaeologists call Old Europe, created craft work in pottery and copper and had a primitive form of writing.

After 3500 B.C., seminomadic groups began moving into the Balkans from the steppe region of what became Russia. These early newcomers were well-organized warriors, using horse-drawn war chariots—the most advanced war technology of the time. They built stone fortresses on the heights above the river valleys. By about 1000 B.C., the strongest of these groups, known as Illyrians, built a powerful kingdom, which survived until a series of conquests by the Romans began in 168 B.C.

Above: **This silver plate, dated A.D. 317, was probably made near Nis, in Serbia. The plate commemorates the 10th anniversary of the Roman emperor Licinius' reign over the Eastern Roman Empire. Licinius (ruled A.D. 308–324) was of Illyrian stock. Historians believe the Illyrians, a rugged mountain people, were the ancestors of modern Albanians.**

Opposite: **The Golubac Castle in Serbia is a spectacular construction that dates back to the second half of the 13th century. Built along the Danube River, the fortress has nine towers.**

AN AGE OF EMPIRES AND MIGRATIONS

Even before the mighty Romans moved in, the Illyrians had felt the humiliation of conquest at the hands of two famous Greek conquerors—first, Philip II of Macedon and then his son, Alexander the Great. They controlled the region for a short time in the mid-300s B.C. The Romans needed nearly two centuries to subdue the Illyrians, finally gaining complete control in A.D. 9. The Illyrians became important to Rome's efforts to protect the empire from outside invaders. The Illyrians were excellent soldiers, and five of their officers rose to become emperors of Rome.

THE ROMAN EMPIRE

One of the Roman emperors, Diocletian, who was struggling to save the empire from waves of invaders, divided the empire in A.D. 285. The division became permanent in A.D. 395, with a boundary along the Sava and Danube rivers. This became a cultural boundary as well as a political one. Rome ruled the lands to the west, and Constantinople ruled lands to the east, known as the Byzantine Empire.

The Romans had a lasting influence on the region. Their genius for engineering and building is still evident in the remains of Roman arenas, roads, aqueducts, and bridges.

For more than a thousand years, great migrations into Europe from Asia altered the course of human history. Waves of people, representing different cultures and ethnic backgrounds, pushed west and southwest from Central Asia. The Romans called these people "barbarians," a Greek word meaning "outsiders or strangers."

One such group, called the Goths, began moving into the Balkans around A.D. 200, slowly forcing the outnumbered Romans to withdraw. Over a period of two or three hundred years, other groups followed the Goths: Huns, Bulgars, Visigoths, Avars, and others.

By the late 400s these invasions had caused the total collapse of the Western Roman Empire. The invaders pillaged and burned as they conquered. They did not respect the advanced culture of Rome, so they thought nothing of destroying beautiful buildings, sculptures, books, or other works of art. With the fall of Rome, Europe entered the Dark Ages. Gradually, these new societies also became civilized, forming kingdoms that were the forerunners of modern nations, including France, England, and Spain. Italy and Germany remained divided into dozens of small kingdoms and principalities until the late 19th century. The Balkans remained splintered even longer.

Opposite: **Dating back to between 520 and 500 B.C., this sculpture of a Greek running girl was found in Prizren, Serbia. Greek conqueror Alexander the Great annexed present-day Serbia to his empire.**

Below: **The remains of a Roman structure can still be seen in present-day Montenegro.**

The Kalemegdan Fortress was built on a strategic location, the junction of the Danube and Sava rivers in Belgrade. Although built on the foundations of a Roman fort, most of the present structure was built by the Austrians in the late 1700s.

THE EMERGENCE OF SERBIA

In the sixth century, another group of tribes, the Slavic people, migrated into the Balkans from the north. Like the other groups, the Slavs lived by farming and herding. They soon gained enough control of the western Balkans to call the area Sclavinia—the Land of the Slavs.

During the Middle Ages, from roughly the 700s to 1300, the Slavs found their lands fought over by several empires: the Franks, Magyars, Bulgars, and the armies of the Byzantine Empire. These empires rose and fell, conquered and withdrew.

Adding to the chaos of the Middle Ages was the failure of any Slavic group to gain control over more than a small area. Practically all of the societies in the region that became Yugoslavia were Slavic, but they were divided into a number of warring tribal groups. Isolated by the mountains and separated by different tribal histories, people felt their strongest loyalty to their village and their large, extended families. Occasionally a strong headman, or *zupan* (ZOO-pahn), would unite several villages and gain power over an area large enough to be considered a kingdom. Slovenia, Croatia, Dalmatia, Bosnia, Herzegovina, and Serbia each experienced a brief golden age as a separate kingdom, before being overwhelmed by powerful empires.

The most important legacy of these short-lived kingdoms was a spirit of nationalism. Centuries later, in the 1800s and 1900s, different Slavic groups looked back to those early kingdoms for an almost mythical history to help prove their legitimacy in forming a nation-state with a home territory and a cultural identity.

In the mid-800s a Serb kingdom emerged under a *zupan* named Vlastimir. Vlastimir acknowledged the overall authority of the Byzantine Empire, but was able to develop a fairly independent kingdom. His relationship with Byzantium encouraged the patriarch of the Eastern Orthodox Church to send two monks, Cyril and Methodius, to teach the Bible to the Serb people. In the process, the two brothers devised a new alphabet, based on the Greek alphabet, known as the Cyrillic alphabet. This is still the alphabet of Serbia and Montenegro, and several other countries, including Russia. Croatia and other countries in the Balkans retain the Roman alphabet, as do most countries in Europe and the Americas.

Over several centuries the Serb kingdom fell to outside conquerors a number of times before emerging again in the early 1300s under King Stephen Dusan. The kingdom flourished for a short time and even dominated much of the Balkan Peninsula. But a new power was rising in the East—the Ottoman Empire.

A statue of St. Cyril and St. Methodius graces a park in Macedonia. The two monks created the Cyrillic alphabet based on the Greek alphabet. The Cyrillic alphabet is still in use in some of the former Yugoslav republics, such as Serbia and Montenegro.

Serbian troops march into the fortress of Uskub during the Balkan Wars in 1911. The first of the wars was fought between the Balkan states and the Ottoman Empire. Uskub is the old name for present-day Skopje, the capital of Macedonia.

THE OTTOMAN EMPIRE

The Ottoman Turks were Muslims. They rose to power gradually and finally gained control of the vast empire of Islam, which stretched from Spain in the west across the Mediterranean and the Middle East to India and Indonesia in the far east. In 1389 they defeated the army of the Serbs at the Battle of Kosovo ("the Field of Blackbirds"). Serbia became a vassal state of the Ottoman Empire, ruled by the Turks until the 19th century.

For nearly 300 years the Serbs continued to resist Ottoman control. Occasionally they found allies in their struggle, such as Russia and the Austro-Hungarian Empire. In 1817 these great European powers forced the Turks to recognize Serbia as an autonomous principality within the empire, with Belgrade as the capital. Complete independence was recognized in 1878.

Over the decades that followed, the Serbs steadily tried to expand their borders. They were also involved in efforts to create a larger Slavic state to include all Slavic peoples, even Poland and Russia. This effort, called Pan-Slavism, was supported by Russia, the largest Slavic state.

In 1912 and 1913, Serbia was involved in two armed conflicts, called the Balkan Wars. The Balkan league (Serbia, Montenegro, Greece, and Bulgaria) conquered Ottoman-held Macedonia and most of Thrace. At the end of these conflicts, the league disagreed on the division of terri-tories. Austria-Hungary and Germany were uneasy about Serbia's increase in power during the Balkan Wars. When the heir to the Austro-Hungarian throne, Archduke Franz Ferdinand, and his wife, were shot and killed by a Serb nationalist, Gavrilo Princip, in Sarajevo on June 28, 1914, Austria-Hungary and Germany reacted severely. The incident sparked off the Great War, or World War I. On July 28, Austria-Hungary declared war on Serbia. Russia then came to the aid of its fellow Slav nation and declared war on Austria-Hungary. The chain reaction of declarations of war continued until all of Europe and much of the world were engulfed in the most terrifying war the world had yet witnessed.

THE ORIGINAL YUGOSLAVIA

When World War I ended in 1918, the victorious Allied powers, including the United States, redrew the map of Europe. Four empires had collapsed during the war—the German, the Austro-Hungarian, the Russian, and the Ottoman; following the idea of self-determination developed by U.S. president Woodrow Wilson, the Allies tried to establish new nation-states that would satisfy the dreams of many ethnic groups who longed for their own national identity.

This photograph shows the assassination of King Alexander I of Yugoslavia by Croatian separatists in Marseille, France, in 1934. The king had been in France on a state visit.

One result of these efforts was the creation of the Kingdom of Serbs, Croatians, and Slovenes, with Peter I of Serbia as king. When Peter's son, Alexander I, came to the throne in 1929, he changed the name of the kingdom to Yugoslavia—the Land of the South Slavs. He also decided to rule as a dictator, in the hope of creating greater national unity. But unity was impossible. The Versailles Treaty recognizing Yugoslavia could not change the geography that left areas in which minority ethnic groups found themselves dominated by the Serb majority. In 1934 King Alexander I was murdered by Croatian terrorists. The king's cousin Paul became regent for the 11-year-old heir, Peter II.

A group of Yugoslav Partisans, guerrilla soldiers recruited by the Communist Party of Yugoslavia, attend the inauguration of the 1st Partisan Brigade in 1941. Led by Marshal Tito, the Partisan Brigades fought against the Axis nations, Germany and Italy, during World War II.

WORLD WAR II AND MARSHAL TITO

World War II (1939–45) was devastating for Yugoslavia. The conflict caused widespread destruction and cost the lives of one in every 10 Yugoslavs. During that same war, a remarkable individual rose to power in Yugoslavia and went on to create, by the force of his rule, a unified state that lasted more than 35 years. His name was Josip Broz, better known as Marshal Tito. Tito was a Communist who rose through the ranks of the Communist Party of Yugoslavia (CPY) in the 1930s and then became the leader of the country's heroic wartime resistance against Nazi Germany.

Early in the war, the Yugoslav government caved in to pressure from Nazi dictator Adolf Hitler and agreed to join the Axis powers (Germany, Italy, and Japan). But the Yugoslav Army rebelled, overthrew the regent

Paul, and placed young Peter II on the throne. Hitler responded by sending an army into Yugoslavia, and when Peter's government fled to England, Hitler divided the country into sections to be ruled by Germany, Italy, and Bulgaria. At the same time, the Croatians formed a neo-Nazi force, the Ustasa, which launched a ruthless campaign of rounding up thousands of Serbs and Jews for execution or for deportation to German concentration camps.

The Germans did not count on the fierce resistance put up by two groups of Yugoslav freedom fighters—the Chetniks, led by Draza Mihailovic, and the Partisans, under Marshal Tito. Even though the two groups fought each other as well as the Germans, the Yugoslav resistance prevented Hitler from gaining complete control of the country. By the end of 1944, with aid from the United States and Great Britain, the freedom fighters had forced the Germans to withdraw.

Marshal Tito signs the declaration that established the Federal People's Republic of Yugoslavia, on March 7, 1945, in Belgrade.

Even during the fighting, Tito had set up local revolutionary councils, and these quickly seized control as the Germans left. In November 1945, Yugoslavia became a republic, with Tito as head of the government. A few months later the Chetniks lost the civil war and Mihailovic was executed by the Tito government.

Tito ruled with an iron hand, maintaining peace among the different ethnic and religious groups. While trying to create a Communist nation, with state control of industry and agriculture, he managed to resist the efforts of the Soviet Union to control all the Communist countries of eastern Europe. Yugoslavia experienced dramatic growth under Tito, but the 1979 worldwide oil crisis led to major economic woes for the country.

MARSHAL TITO

Josip Broz Tito (1892–1980) was one of the great military and political leaders of the 20th century. The first half of his life was characterized by struggle and defeat. As a Communist, he was regarded as a dangerous revolutionary and was imprisoned several times in the 1920s and early 1930s.

During World War II, when he organized the Partisan resistance against Nazi Germany, his heroic stature rapidly emerged. No other country occupied by Germany put up such a spirited resistance as that led by Marshal Tito. Hitler refused to believe that the Partisans could not be defeated, and he committed one army division after another to the task, including a surprise parachute attack that nearly caught Tito. He had to fight his way out of traps several times, and was wounded twice. Still, by 1943 his force numbered 250,000.

After driving the Germans from the country, Tito forged a strong national unity and, during the Cold War, managed to follow a policy of "nonalignment" with either the Soviet-led East or the U.S.-led West. Nevertheless, Tito (*below, center*) welcomed Nikita Khrushchev (*below, left*), Secretary General of the Communist Party of the Soviet Union, and Soviet Prime Minister Nikolai Bulganin (*below, right*) to Belgrade in 1955. He also traveled the world to strengthen Yugoslavia's ties with other nonaligned nations, including India and China.

THE CIVIL WAR

After Tito's death in May 1980, the Communist regime slowly crumbled. In January 1990 the Communist Party gave up control and multiparty elections were held. It now became clear that all the old ethnic, nationalistic, and religious rivalries had only been stifled, not eliminated. In June 1991 Croatia and Slovenia each declared their independence. This immediately led to fighting between Croatians and the ethnic Serbs' military.

When the Serbs in Croatia appealed for help, the Yugoslav Army, largely controlled by Serbia and Serb President Slobodan Milosevic, joined the fighting, plunging Yugoslavia into a long and bloody civil war. The conflict expanded a few months later when Bosnia-Herzegovina also declared independence. Here, too, a Serb minority took up arms against the majority government, which was controlled by Bosnian Muslims, or Bosniaks, and Serbia again sent Yugoslav Army divisions to their aid. In January 1992 Macedonia withdrew from Yugoslavia in a peaceful separation. The two remaining republics in the war-torn country, Serbia and Montenegro, declared themselves to be the Federal Republic of Yugoslavia in April 1992.

The civil war engulfed civilian populations when Milosevic orchestrated a Serb policy of ethnic cleansing. The Serbs, who were members of the Eastern Orthodox Church, were determined to rid the country of Bosniaks and Roman Catholic Croatians. In the vicious campaign thousands of men, women, and children were rounded up. Many were executed and buried in shallow mass graves.

A Croatian man smashes a red star, a symbol of the Communist regime in Yugoslavia, during a street rally in December 1990. In 1991 a group of Serb rebels in Croatia violently opposed the country's separation from Yugoslavia, sparking the civil war.

Residents of Vitina, Kosovo, take to the streets to demand the release of Albanians held in custody in January 2000. A NATO-led force tries to keep the crowds in order.

THE INTERNATIONAL COMMUNITY INTERVENES

News of these horrors leaked out. The United Nations, reflecting outraged world opinion, first imposed economic sanctions on Serbia and then approved the use of troops and warplanes by NATO (North Atlantic Treaty Organization) to stop the fighting. The United Nations also established a War Crimes Tribunal in the Netherlands to investigate charges of "crimes against humanity."

NATO forces managed to stop the fighting, and the Serbs agreed to peace in negotiations held in Dayton, Ohio, at the invitation of U.S. president Bill Clinton. The Dayton Agreement was then signed in Paris in December 1995. Serbia and Montenegro's troubles were far from over, however. Serb President Milosevic refused to accept opposition election victories, and his Serbian government was determined to suppress an independence movement in the province of Kosovo.

KOSOVO

Kosovo was one of two autonomous provinces within the Republic of Serbia. Throughout the 1990s the people of Kosovo agitated for greater independence. About 90 percent of the people were Albanians and they wanted their government to reflect that.

Instead of granting greater independence, Milosevic ordered the Serbian Army into the province in 1999, where it met stiff resistance from the Kosovo Liberation Army (KLA). Frustrated world leaders again searched for a way to restore peace and end the ruthless ambitions of

Milosevic. The United Nations imposed sanctions again. When that failed, NATO warplanes (U.S. and British) launched bombing raids against Serb positions and industries. The 78 straight days of bombing caused heavy damage and forced Milosevic to withdraw his troops.

By this time, well over one million Kosovo Albanians had become refugees, fleeing across the borders into neighboring countries. A UN peacekeeping force moved in, and one of the first steps it took was to oversee elections in September 2000. Milosevic lost the presidential election to Vojislav Kostunica. When Milosevic refused to accept the election results, hundreds of thousands took to the streets in massive public protests. Milosevic finally stepped down in early October and Kostunica was sworn in.

In April 2001, Milosevic surrendered to Serbian authorities. Charged with abuse of power and corruption, he was extradited to the jurisdiction of the International War Crimes Tribunal in the Netherlands to stand trial for encouraging genocide during the civil war.

An ethnic Albanian refugee camp in Macedonia. The civil war displaced more than a million ethnic Albanians from Kosovo.

THE SICK MAN OF EUROPE

For 500 years, the Ottoman Turks (*below*) ruled over a mighty empire. For much of that time, Islam represented the world's most advanced civilization. Kingdoms in Europe gained great advantages from Muslim achievements in science, medicine, astronomy, and other fields. Explorers such as Christopher Columbus would not have been able to sail the world's oceans so freely without the technology and techniques they learned from the Muslims.

In the 1700s the Ottoman Empire entered a long period of decline. Internal weaknesses, combined with the advances in weaponry of European countries, began turning the Ottomans into a second rate military power. In addition, people like the Greeks and Slavs began demanding an end to years of Turkish rule. First, Serbia demanded independence in the early 1800s, followed by Greece in the 1820s. Several times during the 19th century, the great powers of Europe held conferences to decide what to do about the empire they now called "the Sick Man of Europe," sometimes forcing the Ottomans to recognize the independence of one of its provinces.

The end of the empire finally came during World War I. The Turkish leaders sided with the Central powers, led by Germany and Austria-Hungary. When the Allied powers, including England, France, and the United States, won, the Ottoman Empire collapsed and its former provinces either became independent or were made protectorates to be governed by Britain or France.

THE FUTURE OF SERBIA AND MONTENEGRO

Years of turmoil have left Serbia and Montenegro with its economy in ruins, thousands of homeless refugees, and a residue of bitterness among the different ethnic groups. Violence continued in 2004 with some of the worst clashes between Serbs and ethnic Albanians in Kosovo. Again NATO troops were mobilized.

However, with the remarkable courage and resilience that have served the country well during a century of strife, Serbia and Montenegro is rapidly recovering. Financial and other aid from the United States, the United Nations, the European Union (EU), and other agencies is helping to reunite families, find homes for several thousand orphans, and rebuild war-ravaged communities.

Serbian president Slobodan Milosevic (*front row, left*), Croatian president Franjo Tudjman (*front row, center*), and Bosnian president Alija Izetbegovic (*front row, right*) clap after signing the peace agreement on Bosnia, also known as the Dayton Agreement, in Paris, France, on December 14, 1995.

GOVERNMENT

MORE THAN A DECADE OF WAR, political corruption, and economic upheaval made it impossible for Serbia and Montenegro to establish a stable government. Even without that chaos, the loss of four of the six republics that had made up the nation of Yugoslavia required the creation of a completely new national government. At the same time, the people of Kosovo were not anxious to be part of a nation dominated by Serbs.

The upheaval of the 1990s came on the heels of nearly half a century of stability under Marshal Tito and his Communist Party. After Tito's death in May 1980, the communist structure began to crumble. In 1989–90, as communist governments throughout Europe and the Soviet Union rapidly collapsed under the pressure of popular uprisings for freedom, the Communist Party of Yugoslavia gave up power, and multiparty elections were held in 1990.

The future looked bright for a unified government, with each ethnic group having a voice. Two obstacles were to prove overwhelming: the strength of each ethnic group's feelings and the ambitions of Slobodan Milosevic.

In the 1990 elections, each of the new political parties represented a different ethnic, or national, group: Serbs, Croatians, Bosnian Muslims, Macedonians, Slovenes, and Montenegrins. For a unified government to work, each of these groups had to be willing to compromise. The Serbs, however, were anxious to have a dominant role in the new structure, and the Serb president, Milosevic, was eager to make that happen.

Above: **A UN representative greets an observer at a polling station in Pristina in 2001. The elections were the first to be held in Kosovo since the province was placed under the administration of the United Nations.**

Opposite: **The government palace in Belgrade was built in the 1920s. It originally housed the Ministry of Finance of the Kingdom of Yugoslavia.**

NATO soldiers belonging to the Implementation Force (IFOR) monitor the safe return of ethnic Albanians to Kosovo in the German-controlled section.

THE FAILURE OF POLITICS

The people of Croatia and Slovenia were upset by Milosevic's announced plans, which had little to offer the ethnic minorities. Those fears contributed to the decision by both republics to declare their independence in 1991. When Milosevic responded by ordering Serb troops and elements of the Yugoslav army to prevent independence, the civil war was underway. A few months later, Bosnia-Herzegovina and Macedonia also withdrew from Yugoslavia, and that expanded the war. The civil war ended only with the military intervention of NATO, which forced the Serb leader to accept the Dayton Agreement late in 1995.

During the civil war, Milosevic and other leaders had worked out a constitution for Serbia and Montenegro. The document made no mention of the previous status of Kosovo and Vojvodina as autonomous provinces, and there were rumors that Milosevic planned to force Albanians out of Kosovo. The people of Kosovo, nine-tenths of whom were Albanians, formed the Kosovo Liberation Army (KLA) and tried to withdraw from Yugoslavia. Yugoslav army troops retaliated. The fighting stopped after NATO bombing raids forced Milosevic to the negotiating table in 1999. The entire decade of the 1990s had been consumed by ethnic bitterness and the driving ambition of Milosevic. People were eager for a new beginning, and hopes were high for the elections of September 2000. Vojislav Kostunica won the election, but Milosevic refused to accept the result. He had the Federal Constitutional Court nullify the election and name him president.

Serb leader Slobodan Milosevic was arrested and sent to the UN War Crimes Tribunal in The Hague, Netherlands, accused of crimes against humanity, in 2001.

Serbian soldiers cast their votes for a parliamentary election at a polling station in Belgrade in December 2003.

STARTING OVER

Opposition to Milosevic became overwhelming as hundreds of thousands marched through the streets demanding that he step down. In October 2000, the protesters took over parliament and the state-owned television station.

When Russia recognized the presidency of Kostunica the next day, Milosevic finally stepped down. In April 2001, Milosevic was arrested on charges of abusing the office of president and misusing state funds; two months later, he was extradited to the Netherlands to stand trial for war crimes.

In 2001 the new government was finally able to start rebuilding the war-ravaged country and to try to construct a government based on peace among the various groups. Since Croatia, Slovenia, Bosnia-Herzegovina, and Macedonia are now independent states, many sources of friction have now been removed. Even so, Serbia and Montenegro are not united. Minority groups in the two republics are fearful of having their rights suppressed.

In addition, neither Serbs nor Montenegrins were fully satisfied with the new arrangement. In 2002 Serbia and Montenegro began negotiations to forge a looser relationship. In 2003 the country was restructured, with the help of the European Union, into a loose federation of two separate republics. This was done to settle growing demand by Montenegrins for independence.

An agreement was reached that allows either republic to vote on independence—but only after 2006. The issue of Kosovo also remains undecided. As of 2003, UN peacekeepers remained in the province.

THE CRIMES AND THE POPULARITY OF SLOBODAN MILOSEVIC

Milosevic was a bold and ruthless leader. Some people regarded him as a great Serb nationalist; others felt that he was driven only by personal ambition. Whatever the motives, he outraged world opinion during the civil war when he either directed, or simply approved, a plan by Bosnian Serbs to launch a program of ethnic cleansing—removing Bosnia's Muslim minority, either by forcing them to leave or killing them.

People throughout the world were horrified by the news of Serb atrocities. The most outrageous atrocity was probably an incident at Srebrenica in July 1995, in a town the United Nations had designated as a safe zone for Bosniak refugees. Nearly 7,000 unarmed Bosniaks were gunned down as they tried to flee into the forest.

The UN War Crimes Tribunal was established to try those accused of genocide and other crimes against humanity. Milosevic was one of about a hundred government officials and military officers who had been indicted by 2003, but it is reported that several hundred more may still be charged. A few, including a Serb general, have been tried and found guilty. Sentences so far range from five to 30 years. The trials have dragged on slowly, and plans are under way to move the trials to Bosnia for speedier justice.

Even while standing trial, Milosevic has remained immensely popular with nationalistic Serbs (*right*). In general elections held in December 2003, voters elected their former president to a seat in the parliament. Although it is highly unlikely that Milosevic could ever again serve in the government, his strong showing at the polls shows how much support he still has. His Serbian Socialist Party won 22 seats in that election, and the allied Serbian Radical Party won 81 seats, giving the radical nationalists considerable power in the 250-seat parliament.

THE GOVERNMENT STRUCTURE

The parliament of Serbia and Montenegro in session in March 2003. Seated on the front row, from the right, are: Svetozar Marovic, president of Serbia and Montenegro; Vojislav Kostunica, former president of Yugoslavia; Filip Vujanovic, the speaker of parliament; and former Serbian prime minister Zoran Djindjic, who was assassinated in 2003.

The state of Serbia and Montenegro, a republic, has a government that is organized similarly to that of the United States. The federal government is responsible for affairs involving the entire state—the two republics (Serbia and Montenegro) and the two provinces (Kosovo and Vojvodina). In turn, each republic has its own government, much like the individual states in the United States.

The Parliament of Serbia and Montenegro (Savezna Skupstina in Serbian) is divided into two houses: the Council of Citizens (Vece Gradjana) and the Council of Republics (Vece Republika).

The Council of Citizens is the lower house, representing the people much like the U.S. House of Representatives does. Its 138 members are elected for four-year terms, 108 of them elected by Serbian voters, 30 by Montenegrins. The Council of Republics is the upper house, comparable to the U.S. Senate. Half of the 40 members, also serving four-year terms, are elected by Serbs, the other 20 are elected by Montenegrins. The president of Serbia and Montenegro is elected by these two councils.

In addition to the federal government, there are also two national parliaments—one for Serbia and one for Montenegro—and most of the lawmaking functions are carried out by these two parliaments.

The parliament building of Serbia in Belgrade was built in 1907.

The city of Mitrovice in Kosovo has been the site of some of the worst violence in the civil war. NATO forces divided the city into ethnic Serb and Albanian sections.

FEDERAL REPUBLIC DIVISIONS

Serbia and Montenegro each has its own national government consisting of a president, a parliament, and a prime minister. The presidents of Serbia and Montenegro are elected directly by the people for terms of four years.

The members of the Serbian parliament serve four-year terms and elect the prime minister from a list provided by the president. The prime minister then appoints a cabinet to help carry out the duties of the executive branch, such as the treasury, education, and transportation. The government of Montenegro is structured in the same way.

Serbia and Montenegro should now function as semi-independent states within a federal framework. They will conduct their own affairs except for foreign relations, customs, and national defense. Federal power will focus on those three areas, with laws made in the federal parliament.

INTO THE FUTURE

In the early 21st century, it is still difficult to tell where the real executive power will be located. The reason for the confusion is that in the 1990s the president and prime minister of the federation, the prime ministers of the two republics, and the parliaments all became subservient to Milosevic. Now that he has been removed, the power of the personalities in the different executive positions will gradually determine who will be making most of the decisions. The increasing independence of Montenegro should also help to resolve questions of executive power.

The president of Serbia and Montenegro, Svetozar Marovic, was elected in March 2003.

ECONOMY

THE YEARS OF WAR AND UPHEAVAL have had a devastating effect on Serbia and Montenegro's economy. When the nation was made up of six republics, each of the six made contributions to the national economy; the loss of four of those republics has meant that the remaining two—Serbia and Montenegro—have had to find ways to make up for the skills, products, and foodstuffs that previously came from Croatia, Slovenia, Bosnia-Herzegovina, and Macedonia.

For Serbia and Montenegro, the greatest war damage was the result of the NATO bombing raids in 1999. The bombing caused nearly $30 billion worth of damage to oil refineries and factories, along with additional billions of dollars of damage to roads, railroads, and power stations. The economic sanctions imposed on Serbia by the United Nations added to the economic disaster. In the year 2000 slightly more than half the labor force was out of work and inflation continued to skyrocket. Economists predicted that it would take 15 years to restore the country to the prosperity levels of 1989.

Once all sanctions were removed in 2001, when the regime of Slobodan Milosevic was ended, the economy began to show signs of improvement. Serbia and Montenegro is in the beginning phase of economic recovery. Complex political issues, slow development of private enterprise, and a stagnant European economy are hindering progress. It will require years of sustained assistance by international agencies to rebuild homes and restore businesses and farms for tens of thousands of displaced refugees.

Above: **World Bank experts inspect a factory in Nis that produces television sets.**

Opposite: **Many of Serbia's homes were destroyed during the civil war. Home repair is one of the busiest industries today.**

43

Sveti Stefan, an old fishing village located on a rocky peninsula joined to the shore by a sandy strip, has been turned into a luxurious resort hotel.

STATE VERSUS PRIVATE BUSINESS

When Marshal Tito and the Communists came to power in 1945, they started the process of having the government take control of the economy. This was in keeping with the theories of Karl Marx, one of the founders of communism, who wrote that the first step in creating the ideal of communism was to achieve "state ownership of the means of production." State control was achieved quickly, sometimes using force when farm families balked at the idea of collective ownership.

When the Communist government collapsed in 1989, outsiders assumed that there would be a rapid return of factories and farms to private ownership. But it has not happened that way. Many Serbs and Montenegrins seem to prefer having the state own most factories and mines, with workers' councils taking part in managing the facilities. The same is true

44

of large farming areas, where many families are content with a commune-like sharing of ownership.

Some owners of private business complain that the government does not treat them fairly. They say that contracts are rarely awarded to private companies and the tax structure places a heavier burden on them than on the public companies.

The government of Montenegro has made some progress in this task of privatization. In spite of Milosevic's attempts to block their efforts, nearly half of the republic's businesses and farms are in private hands.

THE WORKFORCE

In 2003 roughly 2 million people were employed in the public, or government-run, sector of the economy. Nearly 1.5 million of these were employed in businesses; the rest worked in the service area, including government offices, education, and healthcare services.

UN economists believe that the economy would recover faster if Serbia and Montenegro had more people with 21st-century skills, such as engineering, electronics, and computer science. Thousands who were skilled in these fields were lost in the breakup of the original Yugoslavia, including many who chose to immigrate to other parts of Europe or to North America. In the 1970s, for instance, the state operated a successful automobile-manufacturing company, and its products were exported to Western Europe and North America. But when four of the six republics became independent, Serbia and Montenegro lacked both plants and skilled workers.

An Albanian merchant displays his goods in a shop in Pristina, Kosovo.

AGRICULTURE

Agriculture has always been a major part of Serbia and Montenegro's economy. In fact, until the post-World War II years the great majority of the people made a living farming. Today, agriculture continues to provide more than one-quarter of the gross domestic product (GDP).

About half of the 2 million people employed in state-owned businesses work on large state farms, or collectives. An additional 560,000 own or work on privately owned farms, and another one million people are part-time farmers, growing one or two crops or raising a few animals.

Major agricultural products include corn, sugar beets, wheat, potatoes, plums, and grapes. Dairy cattle, beef cattle, sheep, and pigs are the most important farm animals, along with chickens and geese. The Pannonian Plain in Vojvodina and northern Serbia contains the most fertile farmland, but small farms are scattered throughout the country. In addition, many working families grow grapes for wine, or plum trees for the country's favorite plum brandy.

Forestry also contributes to the economy. Trees are harvested for board lumber and also for wood products such as plywood. However, the lack of laws to protect the environment led to the clear-cutting of steep mountainsides, resulting in landslides and erosion.

MANUFACTURING AND MINING

During the communist years, manufacturing was planned by the state and each republic specialized in certain industries. The breakup of the original Yugoslavia has forced Serbia and Montenegro to start over, building new factories and training workers.

In spite of its many problems, Serbia and Montenegro has the foundations for a productive economy. The country's sources of raw materials include Europe's largest reserves of copper. It also has large deposits of bauxite (for aluminum), coal, lead, and zinc, as well as electrical power potential in the many mountain rivers. The most promising growth industries include iron and steel, textiles, and transportation equipment. In the 1990s, roughly 40 percent of the GDP was provided by industry. That figure declined sharply after the NATO bombing raids, but industrial growth has increased since 2001, in spite of a drop in 2003.

47

Shoppers walk through Republic Square in Belgrade. Since the fall of Communism in the early 1990s, most businesses in Serbia and Montenegro have been privatized.

THE WORKDAY

Business hours are strangely varied, and both foreign visitors and newcomers have to make adjustments. Many businesses and banks open at 7 A.M., for example, and close at 7 P.M.; but some businesses close at noon, then reopen from 4 P.M. until 8 or 9 P.M.

A similar problem occurs on Saturdays. Some business places remain closed, others are open until noon, and still others remain open until late afternoon. The trick for those not familiar with the system is to know when the office or place one is interested in visiting is open.

UNEMPLOYMENT

Hard economic times in any country usually involve high unemployment and runaway inflation. The people of Serbia and Montenegro have been battling these twin problems for more than 20 years. Unemployment probably reached its peak in 1993, in the midst of the civil war, when more than 60 percent of the workforce was out of work. Since then, unemployment rates have fluctuated, but rarely have the numbers dropped below 25 percent unemployed; in 2002, 30 percent of workers were still unemployed.

Inflation has also remained a steady problem, devastating to people on fixed incomes, such as retirement pensions. Inflation was so high in the late 1990s that people joked it was cheaper to paper their walls with money than to buy wallpaper. Economists call this hyperinflation, and they say that the region's inflation rate in the 1990s was the worst in the history of Europe.

Although the introduction of a new currency, called the super dina, was intended to ease inflation, it took time to have any impact. In 2001 inflation was still at 40 percent but dropped to 26 percent the next year, and it was estimated at little more than 10 percent for 2003.

WORKERS IN FOREIGN LANDS

When the economies of western Europe began boom-like growth in the 1970s, thousands of Yugoslav workers headed for West Germany, France, and other countries. Nearly all of these jobs were temporary; therefore many migrant workers lived together in barracks-style housing so they could send more money home. That added income was a boost to Yugoslavia's struggling economy. Between the 1970s and 1990s, roughly one million Yugoslavs were in other European countries and another 110,000 worked in Australia or North America.

A shoeshiner on the streets of Prizren. As unemployment is high in Serbia and Montenegro, many people resort to doing menial tasks to make a living.

ENVIRONMENT

THE LANDS OF SERBIA AND MONTENEGRO offer spectacular natural beauty—from picturesque farms and fishing villages to wild, snowcapped mountains and deep canyons carved by rushing rivers. The region is also one of the most ecologically diverse, with more than 49,000 species of plants and animals cataloged recently.

With the environment, as with all aspects of their life, however, the people face serious difficulties. The troubles began with the pollution produced during the years of Communist rule, and all problems were compounded by the civil war and NATO bombing.

The federal government as well as the national governments of both republics have passed laws intended to repair the damage, but it is too soon to tell if these are working.

Left: **Mount Meded rises above Crno Jezero, or Black Lake, in Durmitor National Park, located on the border between Montenegro and Bosnia-Herzegovina.**

Opposite: **Trees lining the road to the Nemanjina Station have helped to improve the quality of air in the area since they were planted in the 1980s.**

Many buildings in Serbia and Montenegro bear the scars of civil war. Bomb raids on cities such as Kosovo destroyed water and sewage systems and caused terrible environmental problems.

THE LEGACY OF COMMUNISM AND WAR

When the Communists came to power in 1945, they shared the common communist goals of transforming agricultural societies into modern industrial and urban nations. While the regime of Marshal Tito achieved considerable success, the cost amounted to an environmental disaster.

Because the communist planners were so intent on rapid industrialization, they paid no attention to side effects such as air and water pollution. In addition, they used outdated equipment and methods because that was all that was available. Outmoded coal-burning blast furnaces producing iron and steel spewed great clouds of black smoke that hung over the cities. Chemical plants and a new cement industry contributed new combinations of pollutants to the environment. To the communist planners the smog-shrouded factory towns seemed to symbolize industrial progress; in fact, however, the pollutants were poisoning people's lungs, as well as the air, land, and water. The planners insisted that pollution was only a temporary problem, which could be addressed later.

The years of civil war and NATO air strikes also caused widespread damage to the environment. Factories were flattened, mines were flooded, and oil refineries were destroyed, pouring petroleum into rivers and streams. In spite of the widespread damage, large areas of Serbia and Montenegro remain virtually untouched. This is especially true in mountainous regions, where forests and lakes continue to draw tourists and sports enthusiasts from other parts of Europe.

The pristine waters of the Tara Canyon, in Durmitor National Park, attract visitors from all over Europe.

MEASURING THE DAMAGE

In addition to the legacy of communism and war, general lack of environmental awareness has added to the environmental chaos. Farming, for example, has contributed to land and water pollution through the heavy use of chemical fertilizers and pesticides to increase production. The waste leaches into the groundwater, and from there into streams and lakes.

In addition, to increase cropland, the communist planners carried out ambitious programs of building irrigation canals and draining wetland areas in the Pannonian Basin. These efforts did increase farmland, but they also led to increasing salinity (salt content), a common problem with irrigation, and caused erosion and flooding in several areas.

Sewage from urban areas and from cattle and pig farms has further contaminated groundwater with nitrates and phosphates. By the mid-1990s less than 10 percent of Serbia's wastewater was being treated before it was released into the republic's waterways.

The once-magnificent Danube River has suffered enormous damage. Environmentalists point out that this river, one of the longest in Europe, has been like an open sewer flowing through eight countries, serving a population of more than 80 million people. The lake above the Djerdap hydro-electric station has been called the garbage dump of Europe.

Other rivers have been severely damaged. The Sava River has suffered several oil spills, and the Ibar River had such high levels of phenol that the government shut off the water supply from the Kraljevo treatment plant, one of the largest in the Balkans. Air pollution has been as serious a problem as the pollution of land and water. The high sulfur content of coal used in antiquated blast furnaces and in home heating units has had a deadly effect on air quality. Motor vehicle emissions have added significantly to the problem. Few controls have been installed on trucks and buses, and enforcement of laws has been lax.

Opposite: **An oil refinery burns in Novi Sad .**

A SPECIAL ENVIRONMENTAL HAZARD

In some parts of southern Serbia and in Kosovo, there are still numerous signs warning of the danger of land mines (*right*). Thousands of these deadly mines, planted during the war years, still have to be located and detonated.

In December 2001 the UN Interim Administration Mission in Kosovo (UNMIK) determined that minefields had been cleared to internationally acceptable standards. Responsibility for clearing mines was then handed from UNMIK to the Kosovo Protection Corps (KPC). In 2002 the KPC discovered 14 new dangerous areas.

THE IMPACT ON PLANTS AND ANIMALS

Air pollution in the form of acid rain has contributed to the pollution of hundreds of lakes and ponds. These pollutants, including nitrates and phosphates, cause a buildup of algae; the algae growth is more than the ecosystem can handle, leading to a loss of nutrients that kills the algae; decomposing algae choke off the oxygen, resulting in the death of fish and other marine life. The dying off of fish in these lakes and ponds has led to an alarming reduction of birdlife throughout the entire region.

The Balkan region, including Serbia and Montenegro, has been known for varied and unusual plant and animal life. But as of the beginning of the 21st century more than 350 species of plants and animals are listed as

A shepherd leads his flock across a bridge over the Danube River. Shepherds in the former Yugoslavia used to guide their sheep to Bosnia and northern Serbia during the winter months. But since the war, tight border control and landmine-infested roads have made the journey impossible for many shepherds.

endangered. In addition, the years of warfare led many wild animals to seek safety in the mountains of Bulgaria; now that the guns are silent, many of these animals are finding their way back.

EFFORTS TO PROTECT AND RESTORE

Environmental awareness has developed very slowly in Serbia and Montenegro. In the 1980s new laws and a constitutional amendment raised the hopes of environmentalists, as did a growing interest in the so-called Green Movement that was sweeping Europe. This beginning awareness was strengthened in 1988, following the news of the world's worst nuclear accident, at Chernobyl in the Soviet Union. As deadly radioactive clouds drifted westward across Europe no health problems resulted, but the incident made people keenly aware of the fragility of the world's environment and the interconnectedness of its ecosystems.

Since the fighting stopped, the people and the governments of Serbia and Montenegro have shown a new commitment to repairing the damage to the environment and providing better protection in the future. The government of Montenegro, for example, has declared itself to be "the world's first environmental state," with a pledge to live in harmony with nature. The government of Serbia and Montenegro has now signed several international agreements reflecting this new commitment. Seven new nature preserves have been established, along with four new national parks.

Since the late 1990s a number of environmental protection laws have been passed setting up protective standards as well as procedures to guide industries. In addition, a system of ecological permits was established, where a fee is charged—one percent on the value of every new industrial project. Another sign of the new commitment has been the establishment of recycling centers to process industrial wastes.

The people of Serbia and Montenegro are among the world's heaviest smokers of cigarettes. Many women as well as men are chain-smokers, and they insist on their right to light up anywhere, anytime, completely ignoring the many "No smoking" signs.

SERBS AND MONTENEGRINS

THE KINGDOM OF SERBS, CROATS, AND SLOVENES, formed in 1918, changed its name to Yugoslavia in 1929. One of the most striking features of the original Yugoslavia was the great mixing of peoples. This mixing was a source of great cultural richness and diversity. But this diversity also tore the country apart, especially in the late 20th century.

This ethnic and religious diversity has been the product of both history and geography. Century after century, from the time of the ancient Romans, groups migrated into the area from Asia, the Middle East, the Mediterranean lands, and from other parts of Europe. Each group brought its own language, religion, and customs. Once a group had settled in an area, geography came into play, as settlements became isolated from one another by the rugged mountains and deep canyons.

The isolation helped people resist the power of outside invaders and develop a strong sense of independence. It also ensured that over many generations, the beliefs and customs of the culture would become deeply ingrained. Then when others moved into the same area or conquered it, elements of the original culture would survive rather than be submerged.

But after the death of Tito in 1980 Yugoslavia began to break apart along ethnic lines. Serbia, under Milosevic, led various efforts to unite ethnic Serbs into a "Greater Serbia." All such efforts failed.

Above: **A Serbian wears traditional village attire of white shirt, embroidered vest, and cummerband.**

Opposite: **A group of ethnic Albanians return to their home in Kosovo after NATO forces put a stop to the civil war.**

A group of Serbian men stage a protest outside the parliament building, where an electoral committee works on the results of the 2000 election.

THE ETHNIC MIX

The so-called barbarian invasions that continued from about the third century A.D. through the 10th century brought a great variety of tribal groups into the region that became Yugoslavia. By the 600s the earlier barbarian groups, such as the Goths, Huns, and Avars, had moved farther west and a number of South Slavic tribes, including Serbs and Croatians, had come to dominate the region. While these tribal groups shared many physical characteristics and elements of culture, they were often at war with each other. From about A.D. 800, the Serbs controlled much of the region.

Today in Serbia, ethnic Serbs make up about 63 percent of the population; 14 percent are Albanian; 6 percent are Montenegrin; and there are a number of smaller ethnic groups. Montenegro also reveals considerable ethnic mixing, with about 65 percent considering themselves Montenegrins. Other ethnic groups include Slovenes (14 percent), Serbs (9 percent), and Albanians (6.6 percent).

THE RELIGIOUS AND CULTURAL MIX

Conquest of the region by powerful empires has added a variety of peoples and cultures, as well as religions. From the eighth century to the 14th, for example, the Byzantine Empire conquered nearly all of the Balkan Peninsula. The Byzantines brought a highly refined culture to the less advanced Slavic populations, culture that included outstanding architecture, art, and literature.

The Byzantine Empire introduced the Eastern Orthodox church to the Slavs. And to help the Slavic people read and understand the Bible, two monks—Cyril and Methodius—devised the alphabet known as Cyrillic.

The Ottoman Turks moved into the area as the Byzantine Empire declined, conquering most of the Balkans by the 1400s.

The makeup of Serbia and Montenegro reflects the influence of both Byzantium and Islam. In Serbia, about 65 percent of the people belong to the Eastern Orthodox Church—generally called the Serbian Orthodox Church. About 20 percent of the people are Muslim (followers of Islam), and about 4 percent are Roman Catholic.

The mixture of ethnic groups and religions has many regional variations. For instance, in an area that straddles the border between Serbia and Montenegro, a majority of the people are Bosniaks—Muslims who speak the Serbo-Croatian language but write it with the Latin alphabet, not the Cyrillic. The province of Vojvodina is also multiethnic. While about half the people are Serbs, the other half of the people include Hungarians, Croatians, Slovenes, Romanians, and nearly 100 other nationalities.

The Ottomans, the ruling force of Islam, were one of the most advanced civilizations in the world. They excelled in science, mathematics, astronomy, and medicine. Ottoman architectural pieces, like this kiosk, remain in parts of Serbia.

NATIONALISM AND ETHNIC TENSIONS

Nationalism has normally been a force that unites people as they strive to create a nation-state. In the Balkans, however, the land is divided into so many different groups that their nationalistic ambitions often collide.

For several centuries the various groups lived at peace. Ethnic Serbs lived in the same towns or urban neighborhoods as Bosniaks, Croatians, and Slovenes. But nationalist dreams began to emerge in the 1700s, becoming a powerful driving force in the 1800s and 1900s. People were now willing to fight and to die for this ideal of a nation.

The arrival of NATO forces in Kosovo in 1999 prompted many ethnic Serbs to burn their homes and flee the province.

ROMANTIC NATIONALISM

The idea of a nation did not exist through most of human history. People normally accepted being ruled by kings and queens, emperors and empresses, but in the 1700s, as education spread and more people became engaged in business and trade, they wanted to have a greater voice in running their own affairs. People in many societies were inspired by the American Declaration of Independence and the Constitution of the United States.

For many years people could only write and dream about creating their own nation. They wrote books, poems, songs and created artworks depicting their hopes for a time when like-minded people could form their own nation-state. This kind of artistic expression became known as romantic nationalism. This movement inspired classical composers as well. In southeastern Europe, for example, Franz Liszt and Anton Dvorák (*above*) collected folk songs and turned them into stirring national anthems and songs.

When the former Yugoslavia was formed in 1918 (first as the Kingdom of the Serbs, Croats, and Slovenes), it did not really answer the strong nationalist ambitions of the different groups. In an effort to satisfy those ambitions, the federation was made up of six republics: Serbia, Croatia, Slovenia, Bosnia-Herzegovina, Montenegro, and Macedonia, plus the two autonomous provinces of Kosovo and Vojvodina. One reason that this arrangement was not more successful was that Serbia, the largest of the republics, tended to dominate the government. People in the other republics resented the Serb power and often feared that their republic would be swallowed up. The Serbs, in turn, were uneasy about border areas, where a local minority of Bosniaks or Croatians might want to join a neighboring republic.

While Tito's Communist government managed to maintain peace and stability, the force of nationalism again became dominant in the 1990s. First the Slovenes, then the Croatians pulled away, followed by Bosnia, Herzegovina, and Macedonia. More trouble erupted when the people of Kosovo, nine-tenths of whom were ethnic Albanians, took up arms in 1998 rather than yield to the power abuses of the Serbian police and military.

ETHNIC REFUGEES

The warfare of the 1990s displaced more than 2 million people, and several thousand are still in relocation camps or are trying to settle with people of the same ethnic background or religion. In the mid-1990s, for example, an estimated 640,000 refugees fled to Serbia from Croatia and Bosnia. Then during the fighting in Kosovo in 1998–99, another 600,000 people were on the move, and this time the refugees were mostly ethnic Albanians who fled to Albania, Macedonia, or Montenegro. When the NATO peacekeeping force moved in, the refugees began to return.

Once the NATO force had taken control of Kosovo, they ordered all Serbian government workers and police to leave the province. The Serb civilians who remained found that resentment against them was so strong that they no longer felt safe or comfortable living there.

At the start of the 21st century an estimated 200,000 Serb refugees had relocated to Belgrade or the province of Vojvodina. Officials of the UN Refugee and Relief Administration are hopeful that the massive movement of people has now ended and that the last refugee camps will be emptied by 2005.

THE PRINCE AND THE POET

One of the great heroes of Yugoslavia's history was a Montenegrin named Petar II Petrovic Njegos (*right*)—a unique individual who was a bishop, a prince, and an outstanding poet.

Born in Montenegro, Njegos belonged to a clan of leaders. Like others in his family, he became both a bishop of the Eastern Orthodox Church and a ruler of Montenegro. When his uncle died in 1830, the clan made him prince, or ruler, at the age of seventeen. Njegos ruled, improving the government and the economy, until his untimely death in 1851.

Njegos is best known today as an outstanding poet. His most famous poem was *The Mountain Wreath*, and another long poem, *The Ray of the Microcosm*, is said to be one of the country's great philosophical statements.

TWO SPECIAL MINORITIES

Two small minority groups—the Roma, who are the people formerly known as Gypsies, and the Jews—suffered terribly in World War II. Thousands were rounded up by Nazi troops and by the Croatian neo-Nazi Ustasa and shipped to Nazi death camps.

Many of Yugoslavia's Jews came as refugees from Spain in 1492, the year that Christopher Columbus made his historic voyage. The newcomers added valuable elements to the region's culture, especially in professions such as law, education, and medicine. Only a few thousand of those who survived the war decided to remain in Yugoslavia.

The Roma of the Balkan Peninsula may have numbered one million people in 1939, when World War II began. Roughly half that number—an estimated 400,000—died in Nazi labor camps and gas chambers.

The Roma were originally from northern India, and it is believed they migrated to the West in the 1100s, spreading throughout Europe. The few thousand who remain in Serbia and Montenegro continue to live on the fringes of society as fortune-tellers, circus performers, horse traders, and jewelry makers.

Opposite: **A Romany youth earns some pocket money by cleaning the windshield of a tram in Belgrade. The Romany, or Gypsy, originated in northern India but settled in many parts of Eastern Europe and the Middle East.**

LIFESTYLE

FOR MOST OF ITS HISTORY, Yugoslavia was primarily a rural, agricultural society. Cities and towns had existed since Roman times, but they remained small and contained only a fraction of the population.

Industry began to develop in the 20th century, especially after the Communists took control in 1945. The needs of industry led to a steady migration of people from farms to cities and towns. Still, by 1980 only about one-third of the population lived in urban areas.

At the beginning of the 21st century that figure reached 52 percent, meaning that for the first time, more than half the people lived in cities and towns. Although the process of urbanization and industrialization was slowed by the years of war, the change from rural to urban in lifestyle should now begin to speed up again.

Left: **After a decade of civil war, ethnic conflict, and economic sanctions, Serbs and Montenegrins are now able to enjoy relative peace and stability.**

Opposite: **Serbian and Montenegrin children play in the courtyard of an old town in the historic area of Montenegro.**

RURAL LIFE

The way of life in rural areas differs a good deal from region to region. The province of Vojvodina, for example, is located on the broad Pannonian Plain—a fertile land crisscrossed by rivers, making it the country's best farmland. The farms are large and generally prosperous, with broad fields of grains such as wheat and oats, along with orchards of plums and apples, as well as grapevines for making wine.

Villages in Vojvodina are generally large and far apart. Some larger towns, with between 5,000 and 10,000 people, are big enough to be considered urban, but they remain basically rural, serving the marketing and distribution needs of several farm villages. Some clusters of homes are surrounded by a wall or fence, often with a very ornate gate leading to a center courtyard, which provides some privacy.

An unusual feature of Vojvodina is the appearance of isolated farms that look like the remote homesteads of the American Great Plains of the 19th century. These scattered homesteads started as *tanyaks* (TUN-yucks)—harvest shelters built in the late 1800s, when there was no longer a danger from marauding Turkish armies.

By contrast, rural life in Kosovo, the other province, is much harder. Roughly half the land is mountainous and forested. The rest is best for grazing or for growing hardy grains. It is a poor land, where families scramble to coax a living out of the thin, rocky soil. In the past the need for protection led to the building of houses around a square, surrounded by a mud wall. Towers at the corners, called *kula* (KU-la) houses, looked much like American pioneer blockhouses, with no windows on the ground floor.

In the hilly regions of Serbia, small farm villages appear along the roads that follow the crest of hills. The houses, built close together, are mostly constructed of logs or rough-hewn planks, with shingle roofs, and often plaster walls.

Rural life is also hard in Montenegro, and there is simply not enough land to support the population. Mountain shepherds continue to roam the hills searching for good pasture and protecting their flocks from wolves and other predators. Some say that the hard life is reflected in the Montenegrins' somber national costume of red, black, and gold and in the almost mournful cries of their folk songs.

Other observers say that the most important aspect of the Montenegrin character is the spirited sense of independence. For 500 years Montenegro was the only part of the Balkans that the Ottoman Turks never subdued. As a symbol of their defiance, one can point to the railings of the Vlaska Church in the town of Cetinje, which were made out of rifle barrels seized from Ottoman Turk soldiers in one of their many battles.

Older Serbian men enjoy a game of chess on the Danube's riverbank.

69

LIFE IN BELGRADE

At the end of World War II, only about one-quarter of Yugoslavia's people lived in urban areas. Over the next 45 years, the poverty of farm life in much of the country led people to migrate to Belgrade and other developed areas. The rapid industrialization under the Communists seemed to offer a better way of life. By the late 1980s nearly half the population lived in cities and large towns.

Belgrade is the capital of Serbia and Montenegro and by far its largest city, with about 15 percent of the country's population. The city is an intriguing combination of the very old and the new, a city of fascinating images, such as a sleek Italian sports car parked in front of a thousand-year-old Eastern Orthodox church, or the glass wall of a modern office building reflecting Kalemegdan Citadel, a solid 17th-century fortress looming over the "old town."

The old town itself, a neighborhood called Stari Grad, is testimony to Belgrade's long history. The city dates back to the Illyrians in the fourth century B.C., and in its 2,500 years it has been destroyed and rebuilt more than 40 times. Serbs and Montenegrins are proud of their history, and many enjoy pointing out evidence of that history, such as a medieval gate, the tomb of a Muslim ruler, or Turkish public baths built in the 1500s.

Downtown Belgrade bustles with activity, with traffic jams and sidewalks crowded with office workers, shoppers, and tourists. The busy center of the city is Kneza Mihailova—a pedestrian boulevard lined with stores, coffee shops, and cafés with outdoor tables. Business people discuss deals while sipping thick Turkish coffee, and well-dressed patrons fill expensive restaurants, giving the city a sophisticated air not unlike Paris or Rome. Across the Sava River from downtown is "New Belgrade," an area of newer government buildings and apartment complexes.

Many of the buildings constructed during the Communist years are big steel and concrete structures with few windows and little style. Some of the gigantic apartment blocs could house 10,000 people—a size designed to give Communist authorities maximum control. The people have never liked these huge structures—they call them silos for sleeping—and many are now being replaced by modern urban housing.

Most urban Serbians live in apartment blocks like these ones in Podgorica, Montenegro.

VARIATIONS IN RURAL STYLES

There are sharp differences in lifestyle between the countryside and the cities. Rural life is slower, and people are more conservative, or traditional, in their tastes and values. In clothing styles, for example, many rural women now wear Western-style clothing, but others prefer their national costume—that is, the traditional outfit of an ethnic group or a geographic region.

These styles differ from region to region. Rural Serbian women wear ankle-length dresses covered by a short apron decorated with embroidery; they also wear heavy gold jewelry and head scarves that hang down in back. In Muslim villages, women usually wear baggy trousers gathered at the ankles and aprons embroidered in rich and vibrant colors. In city areas, these traditional styles are usually worn only on festive occasions.

In the rural areas of Serbia and Montenegro, many people are engaged in agriculture and animal farming. This cattle market is located in Vojvodina, a province in northern Serbia, an area known for its fertile agricultural land.

VARIATIONS IN URBAN LIFE

City life also shows regional variations. Novi Sad is a university town that seems unusually open and friendly, proud of the diversity of its people. Roughly 20 percent of the people are Hungarian, and there are reported to be 100 different national and ethnic groups in the city —Croatians, Slovenes, Bosniaks, Macedonians, Greeks, Bulgarians, and so on. Radio Novi Sad broadcasts in Serbian, Hungarian, Slovakian, and Romanian.

Novi Sad is a picturesque city nestled in a curve of the Danube, its ancient buildings and tiled roofs giving it the feeling of a medieval town. On weekends and in the evenings, couples and families stroll along the walls of the Petrovaradin Citadel, an elegant fortress built in the 1800s. It is also an important port on the busy Danube, transporting goods to Budapest and beyond.

Budva, on the Adriatic, is a beach resort with a more relaxed lifestyle. The "old town" was almost totally demolished in a 1979 earthquake, but it has been rebuilt with painstaking care. The town square, the churches, and the fortress all have the picturesque appearance of a movie set, drawing tourists back to the coast.

A few miles south of Budva is Sveti Stefan, which was once a small fishing village. The old stone cottages, with red tile roofs, are now available as luxurious rentals. Cetinje, once the capital of Montenegro, has the aura of a citadel, which in fact it was—an impregnable fortress-city that resisted the armies of the Ottoman Turks for 500 years. Residents and visitors enjoy the narrow winding streets and the romantic old buildings.

A few miles south of Budva is Sveti Stefan. Once a small fishing village, Sveti Stefan was abandoned by the fishing families after World War II, but it has been redeveloped, and a causeway connects it to the mainland. Fishermen have returned to the village, but they now cater mostly to the needs of tourists.

FAMILY

The people of Serbia and Montenegro have a strong sense of family. Patterns of kinship, or extended family, are important in many areas of life. At weddings and other family gatherings, an individual is likely to know forty or fifty family members—aunts, uncles, cousins, and so on. Someone seeking a job will mention family ties, and this can be a decisive factor. A custom called *kumstvo* (KUM-stvo) is also common. This is a form of family sponsorship with formal ties that continue through a person's life.

In some regions, especially Montenegro, people live in large family

Families are close-knit and often include the members of the extended family. This family in Gracanica, Kosovo, consists of parents, children, and grandparents.

groups. Relationships are close and intense. Usually these close-knit families enable children to grow up with a strong sense of security. One negative aspect of clan life is that an insult to a clan member can fester for years and can sometimes lead to feuds that continue for generations.

EDUCATION

Schooling is free and compulsory for children ages 7 to 14, and it is free and voluntary for secondary school. As recently as 1998, however, enrollment was low, with only 70 percent of those eligible actually in school. In addition, literacy rates are not equal, with 89 percent of women classified as literate and 98 percent of men. Both literacy and enrollment rates are lower for ethnic Albanians than for other groups.

Ethnic Albanians faced special educational difficulties in 1990, when Serbian authorities closed schools they said were teaching too much about Albania. To get around the government's demand for a uniform state curriculum, Kosovar Albanians set up "underground schools" in private homes, but the quality of this schooling tended to be mediocre. In 1999, when the UN Peacekeeping Force created a more stable government, the system began to improve.

There are several universities in Serbia and Montenegro. The University of Belgrade, founded in 1863, is the oldest; others are located at Kragujevac, Novi Sad, Nis, Podgorica, and Pristina.

The higher education system, already weakened by these disputes, was damaged further in 1998, when the Serb parliament placed all universities under direct government control. This put severe limits on academic freedom, especially after several prominent professors were fired. It seems likely that the fall of Slobodan Milosevic will lead to a restoration of that freedom.

The University of Pristina was forced to close in the 1990s, after its ethnic Albanian faculty members were dismissed. Some faculty members continued to operate on an underground basis until the school was reopened in 2000 as an Albanian university. Serbian authorities responded by opening a Serbs-only university nearby.

RELIGION

RELIGION HAS BEEN A POWERFUL FORCE in the history of eastern Europe—sometimes as a unifying force, but other times as a very divisive one. In spite of this importance, most Serbs and Montenegrins do not seem to practice their religion with great devotion. One recent study found that only about 10 percent of the people attend their church or mosque regularly. Older people, especially in rural areas, appear to be much more devout.

During the Communist years the government was hostile toward organized religion at first, but then became more tolerant. The rise of strong nationalistic feelings in the 1980s and 1990s created a new interest in religion, and this is when it most recently proved to be both a unifying and a divisive force. Religion unified when it supported nationalistic hopes and dreams.

During the civil war of the 1990s, the ethnic Serbs were identified with the Eastern Orthodox Church. They considered those of different religions to be their enemies, namely Muslims and Roman Catholics.

Left: **Prizren, a town in Kosovo, bears the signs of Serbia's past rulers. The Sinan Pacha mosque (*foreground*) was built in 1615 by the Ottoman rulers; while the monastery of St. Spas (*background*), or St. Savior, was built in the 1300s by Slavic kings on the slopes of the Sharr Mountains.**

Opposite: **The monastery of St. Peter in Cetinje, Montenegro, was built in 1701. The archway is decorated with a fresco depicting icons of the Orthodox Church.**

CATHOLIC AND ORTHODOX CHURCHES

The Eastern Orthodox Church and the Roman Catholic Church were originally the two main branches of Christianity. When the Roman Empire was divided into West (still called the Roman Empire) and East, the Eastern Empire became known as the Byzantine Empire, with its capital at Constantinople.

A Serbian Orthodox priest blesses two of the faithful during an Easter service at St. Petka Church in Belgrade.

In the centuries that followed, the two churches steadily grew farther apart, especially over a controversy involving interpretation of the Holy Trinity (Father, Son, and Holy Ghost). The pope in Rome was the head of the Roman Catholic Church. In the East, the bishop, or patriarch, of Constantinople was officially the head of the Eastern Orthodox Church, but in practice, each national church has exercised a good deal of independence. This independence is reflected in the names of some national churches, such as the Serbian Orthodox Church, the Greek Orthodox Church, and the Russian Orthodox Church.

The service of the Eastern Orthodox Church also developed in different ways. It is a much more elaborate service, with a strong appeal to the senses through the haunting chants of the music, the heavy smell of incense, and the visual image of many icons (paintings of religious figures, such as the saints and the holy family).

THE APOSTLES OF THE SLAVS

Two brothers played an important part in the development of both the religion and language of the Yugoslav region. Both Cyril (827–869) and

Methodius (825–884) were brilliant scholars, specializing in theology and language. In A.D. 863 the patriarch of Constantinople sent them to convert the Slavic tribes to Christianity. In order to teach the holy scriptures (the Bible), they used the Slavonic language. Since there was no written form of the language, the brothers invented an alphabet, built on Slavonic sounds and based on the Greek alphabet. This alphabet, called Cyrillic, is still used in Serbia, Macedonia, Russia, and several other countries. Originally, the Cyrillic alphabet required 43 characters to cover the richness of the Slavonic sounds, but modifications have reduced the number to 30 letters (32 in Russia).

For their great contributions, the brothers became known as the Apostles of the Slavs, and they were made saints in both the Catholic and Orthodox churches. (Their feast day is celebrated on February 14 in the Roman Catholic Church and May 11 in the Eastern Orthodox Church.)

Serbian Orthodox Christians light candles inside St. Petka Church in Belgrade during an Easter service.

MOTHER TO THE WORLD

Gonxha Agnes Bojaxhiu (*left*) was born in 1910 to Albanian parents, grew up in Yugoslavia, and then took her vows as a nun with the name Teresa. Sister Teresa moved to India, where she became a teacher and, later, a school principal.

In 1946 she responded to an inner calling to help the poor and moved into the poorest slums of Calcutta. She became known as Mother Teresa and gathered others around her to help the poorest and the sickest—the people ignored and discarded by society. Her fame spread throughout the world, and in 1979 she was awarded the Nobel Peace Prize. She died in 1997. In 2003 the Roman Catholic Church began the process to canonize her as Saint Teresa—a small, frail woman who saved thousands and inspired millions.

MINORITY RELIGIONS

The original Yugoslavia that existed from 1919 to 1990 was a great mixture of religious, ethnic, and linguistic groups. In the six constituent republics, Roman Catholics formed the largest group in Croatia and Slovenia; Muslims were a majority in Bosnia and Herzegovina; and the Eastern Orthodox religion was dominant in Serbia, Montenegro, and Macedonia.

The new nation of Serbia and Montenegro is much less diverse. More than 65 percent of the people are Eastern Orthodox, about 19 percent are Muslim, 4 percent are Roman Catholic, and the remaining 12 percent are Protestant or other religions, including Jews, who make up less than one percent of the population.

THE EASTERN ORTHODOX CHURCH AND NATIONALISM

During the centuries of Turkish rule, some Serbs converted to Islam because they knew that as Muslims, they would have greater opportunities in business and government. Those who remained in the Eastern Orthodox Church were exposed to discrimination. Some expressions of prejudice were merely nuisances. For instance, when a Muslim rode by on horseback, a Serb rider was expected to dismount and wait for the rider to pass. Other manifestations of prejudice were more troublesome, such as paying higher taxes or being forbidden to live in certain neighborhoods.

Centuries later, during the civil war of the 1990s, Serb soldiers inflicted grim revenge on the Bosniaks who became their prisoners. They felt it was a justified payback for the humiliation inflicted on their families by the Ottoman Turks—an indication of the depth of ethnic bitterness.

For most Serbs and Montenegrins, the Eastern Orthodox Church was a safe haven and a source of strength during the years of Turkish rule, from 1389 to 1878. The church enabled people to retain their national identity. They held secret meetings in the churches and even planned armed uprisings against the occupying armies. The clandestine meetings helped the tough fighters of Montenegro avoid a complete Turkish conquest. And from 1482, Montenegro was ruled from Cetinje by leaders called *vladike* (vla-DEE-ke)—bishops in the Eastern Orthodox Church.

Ethnic Albanians gather at a Roman Catholic church in Pristina, Kosovo, to attend a mass offered for the sake of peace in the war-stricken province in March 1998. A man weeps, while a young girl holds a picture of Mother Teresa.

ISLAM

Roughly 20 percent of the population of Serbia and Montenegro is Muslim—followers of Islam. Islam is one of the world's great religions, founded by the Prophet Muhammad in the seventh century A.D. It is a monotheistic (belief in one God) religion, and Muslims accept some portions of both Judaism and Christianity. Muslims, for example, accept Abraham, Moses, and Jesus as great prophets, but Muhammad is considered the last and greatest of the prophets.

The Five Pillars of Islam, to be followed by all the faithful, include answering the five daily calls to prayer. The call is given by a *mussein*

Muslim men gather to pray at a mosque in Pristina, Kosovo.

A NEW "CRIME AGAINST HUMANITY"

The power of ethnic/religious hatred was revealed during the civil war in the brutality of Serb atrocities against Bosniaks. In Serb concentration camps, thousands of Muslim women (*right*) and shockingly young girls were systematically raped and often made pregnant. The Serb soldiers knew that in Muslim cultures, victims of rape were regarded as unclean and would not be accepted back into the village or family.

In the war crime trials still being conducted at The Hague in the Netherlands, the judges declared that rape, like ethnic cleansing, would now be considered a crime against humanity. In Serbia and in Bosnia, UN medical and psychiatric workers are trying to help families accept victims back into the community.

(MOOSE-eyn), usually from a tower called a minaret. In Muslim neighborhoods, prayer takes place in a mosque. If a mosque is not available, Muslims kneel on a small prayer rug facing the holy city of Mecca. Another of the Five Pillars is to observe the holy month of Ramadan by fasting and praying each day from dawn to sunset. Almost 20 percent of Montenegrins are Muslims who live in the Sandzak region. Ethnic Albanian Muslims live in the area bordering Albania as well as in Kosovo.

For centuries the Balkan people of the various religions coexisted. In fact, in many towns and city neighborhoods, Roman Catholics, Eastern Orthodox Christians, and Muslims were proud of the diversity, often sharing the same neighborhood. And in the decades before the civil war, there was a growing acceptance of intermarriage. The powerful force of nationalism unleashed the submerged fears and resentment that had lurked beneath the surface, and the resulting explosion of hatred was expressed in terms of religion.

LANGUAGE

THE GREAT MAJORITY OF PEOPLE who settled present-day Serbia and Montenegro were Slavic. The diversity that emerged, and that eventually tore the country apart, was based on religion and language rather than on different physical characteristics. The people of Serbia and Montenegro belong to the Eastern Orthodox Church, while most Bosnians are Muslims, and Croatians are Roman Catholics. The language of all three is Serbo-Croatian, although in Serbia, the language is officially called Serbian. A more important distinction is that Serbs use the Cyrillic alphabet, while Croatians use the Roman.

ONE LANGUAGE, TWO ALPHABETS

In A.D. 863, two brothers—Cyril and Methodius—were sent to the Czech lands by the patriarch of the Eastern Orthodox Church. The two monks were brilliant scholars and linguists, and their mission was to Christianize the southern Slavs. To acquaint the Slavic-speaking peoples with the Bible, they invented an alphabet, now called Cyrillic, based on the Greek alphabet. Since Slavic languages were rich in sounds, the brothers found they needed 43 letters, a number that has since been reduced.

The brothers were made saints in both the Eastern Orthodox and Roman Catholic branches of Christianity for Christianizing many Slavic peoples and for influencing the cultural development of those peoples. Together, Saint Cyril and Saint Methodius have the title of the Apostles of the Slavs.

Above: **This panel, made of carved bone and wood in the late 1700s, shows the Cyrillic alphabet.**

Opposite: **Serbian newspapers and magazines, written in both the Roman and Cyrillic scripts, are sold at a stall in Belgrade.**

LANGUAGE VARIATIONS

The division between the Croatian and Serbian languages originated in the 11th century when both groups converted to Christianity. The Serbs were aligned with the Eastern Orthodox Church, which used the Cyrillic alphabet. The Croats followed the Roman Catholic Church and its eventual use of the Latin alphabet. In the 19th century, Vuk Stefanovic Karadzic simplified the Serbian language.

In most areas of Serbia and Montenegro, the majority of people are Slavs who speak the Serbian language and use the Cyrillic alphabet. However, there are some regional variations. Near Serbia's border with Bosnia-Herzegovina, for example, the majority of the people are Bosniaks. They speak the Serbian language, but they usually call it Serbo-Croatian, and they write it in the Roman (or Latin) script.

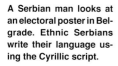

A Serbian man looks at an electoral poster in Belgrade. Ethnic Serbians write their language using the Cyrillic script.

A bookstore in Belgrade's prime shopping district. Kneza Mihailova.

Ethnic Albanians form a majority in several areas of Kosovo, one of the country's two autonomous provinces. Most of these people are Muslims, but to add to the confusion, large numbers are Orthodox Christians and smaller numbers are Roman Catholic. All speak Albanian and use the Roman alphabet.

In the other province—Vojvodina—Hungarians are a majority in a number of towns and villages. Most speak both Hungarian and Serbian; many use the Roman alphabet, although they are able to read the Cyrillic script, at least for such practical things as street signs.

Most people in Serbia and Montenegro have at least a casual knowledge of a second language. For many, that language is German, a legacy of the 1970s and 1980s, when thousands of Yugoslav workers lived temporarily in West Germany, where the economy was humming and the workers could send most of their earnings home to what was then Yugoslavia. English is also a popular second language, especially among young people.

LANGUAGE REFORMER: STEFANOVIC KARADZIC

Vuk Stefanovic Karadzic (1787–1864), (*bottom*), was both a hero of Serb nationalism and a brilliant scholar who improved and simplified the Serbian language. In addition, he was the country's greatest collector of folk songs and stories.

As a Serbian patriot, Karadzic took part in the first uprising against the Ottoman Turks, in 1804. One of his duties was to read and write for the Serb commanders, most of whom were illiterate. After several years of revolution, he was forced to flee. He went to Vienna where he became known as an outstanding scholar.

Karadzic began collecting popular songs and poems, but he was troubled by inconsistencies in the Cyrillic script, especially a duplication of sounds. He discovered that the Serbian language contained thirty sounds, but the Cyrillic alphabet had no letters for six of them.

He created new symbols and discarded 18 others that were not needed. In 1818 he published his *Serbian Lexicon* (*Srpski rjecnik*), which was updated in 1852 to more than 46,000 words. Many church officials objected to the drastic changes, but the new alphabet was so simple and effective that the opposition soon disappeared. The lexicon (dictionary), which includes valuable information about folklore, is still a classic.

Karadzic also made important contributions to Yugoslavia's folklore.

SILENT LANGUAGE

People in every culture communicate in a variety of nonverbal ways, such as hand gestures, facial expressions, and actions. Anthropologist Edward Hall called this the "silent language." Hall pointed out that the silent language often conveys messages that are not intended or that are misinterpreted.

For example, a former member of the UN Peacekeeping Force in Kosovo was disturbed because Serbian officials were always 10 to 15 minutes late for meetings. The official concluded that "the Serbs don't respect the United Nations mission." He did not know that in Serbian culture it is considered proper to be 10 minutes late for a meeting; arriving sooner is regarded as being too aggressive.

Another example of the silent language is the use of hand gestures and facial expressions. Tourists sometimes think that a café discussion is a heated argument with the participants about to fight; in fact, the speakers are usually just expressing themselves vigorously.

Yugoslavs like to use hand gestures when they speak to one another.

PRONUNCIATION

The writing systems of Serbian are phonetic—that is, every letter is pronounced and the sound represented by that letter does not change from word to word. There is some variation in where the stress is placed in a word, but the one general rule is that the stress, or accent, is never on the last syllable, and in most words it is on the first vowel.

English letters	Cyrillic	Pronunciation	English letters	Cyrillic	Pronunciation
Aa	Аа	a in f<u>a</u>ther	Ll	Лл	l in <u>l</u>eg
Bb	Бб	b in <u>b</u>ed	Mm	Мм	m in <u>m</u>oon
Cc	Цц	ts in ca<u>ts</u>	Nn	Нн	n in <u>n</u>ight
Dd	Дд	d in <u>d</u>oor	Oo	Оо	o in <u>o</u>pen
Ee	Ее	e in b<u>e</u>t	Pp	Пп	p in <u>p</u>age
Ff	Фф	f in <u>f</u>ire	Rr	Рр	r in <u>r</u>oom
Gg	Гг	g in <u>g</u>oose	Ss	Сс	s in <u>s</u>un
Hh	Хх	h in <u>h</u>uman	Tt	Тт	t in <u>t</u>ime
Ii	Ии	ee in n<u>ee</u>d	Uu	Уу	oo in sp<u>oo</u>n
Jj	Јј	y in <u>y</u>es	Vv	Вв	v in <u>v</u>an
Kk	Кк	k in <u>k</u>id	Zz	Зз	z in <u>z</u>ulu

A number of letters and pairs of letters have special sounds, especially when there is an accent mark. Here are some of the special pronunciations:

Latin script	Cyrillic	Pronunciation	Latin script	Cyrillic	Pronunciation
Čč	Чч	<u>ch</u>eese	Šš	Шш	sh in <u>sh</u>ip
Dž dž	Џџ	jeep	Žž	Жж	s in vi<u>s</u>ion
Ćć	Ћћ	la<u>tch</u>	Lj lj	Љљ	li in mi<u>ll</u>ion
Đđ	Ђђ	ba<u>dge</u>	Nj nj	Њњ	ny in ca<u>ny</u>on

SOME SAMPLE WORDS AND PHRASES

English	Serbian	Pronounced
Hello	*Zdravo*	ZDRAH-VO
Good-bye	*Dovidjenja*	DP-VEE-dyEH-nyAH
Yes	*Da*	DAH
No	*Ne*	NEH
Please	*Molim*	MOH-leem
Thank you	*Hvala*	HVAH-lah
Excuse me (Sorry)	*Oprostite*	OH-proh-steet
What's your name?	*Kako se zovete?*	KAH-koh SEH ZOO-veht-eh?
My name is. . .	*Zovem se . . .*	ZOH-vehm SEH
Do you speak English?	*Govorite li Engleski?*	GO-vor-ee-the lee ehn-GLEH-skee
Where is…	*Gde je…*	GDEH YEH
one	*jedan*	YEH-dahn
ten	*deset*	DEH-seht
twenty	*dadeset*	DVAH-deh-seht

ARTS

A NUMBER OF THEMES run through all forms of the arts in Serbia and Montenegro. One of these influences is the long folk history of the people and of the different ethnic and religious groups. Modern music draws on the folk music of the past; for example, novels and poems build on historic themes, and even modern abstract paintings echo themes from long ago.

A second recurring theme, and one that is related to the folk history, is the struggle, drama, and tragedy of the country's history. Novels, poems, and short stories explore the centuries of warfare waged against the Turks, then the Austrians and Hungarians, and then the Germans in World War II—conflicts that often ended in tragedy.

A third influence on the arts has been the Eastern Orthodox Church, particularly in the early development of the arts. From about A.D. 1000 to 1400, the architecture and decorations of the churches represented outstanding contributions to art. Poetry and painting also dealt with religious themes, at least until influences from western Europe began to be felt in the mid-1800s. These later influences involved first the romantic era of heroic paintings and poetry, then the impressionism of the late 1800s.

The 20th century saw the destruction of many cultural monuments and artifacts. The Institute for the Protection of Cultural Monuments was created in 1947 to identify, study, and protect Serbia's "cultural property."

Belgrade is the cultural center of Serbia, with dozens of cultural institutions.

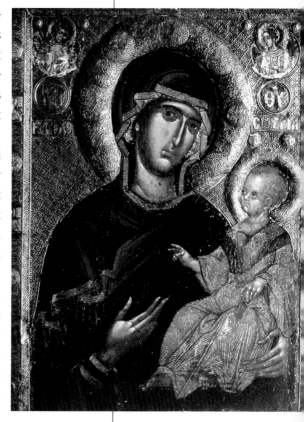

Above: **This Byzantine icon of the Virgin Mary, Savior of Souls, was created in Serbia in the 14th century.**

Opposite: **The magnificent Ostrog Monastery was built in the 1600s on a hill near Niksic, Montenegro.**

The public square in the old town of Petrovaradin has been beautifully restored, after it was badly damaged by NATO bombing in 1999. The town's historical structures were mostly built in the 1600s and include a castle, a fortress, a church, and a Catholic convent.

THE CHURCH AND THE ARTS

The most famous artworks in Serbia and Montenegro are beautiful frescoes (wall paintings) produced in the 13th and 14th centuries in Orthodox churches scattered throughout the mountains and valleys. The Patrijarsija Monastery near Pec, for example, contains three 13th century churches, each displaying magnificent medieval frescoes beneath their domed roofs. And just a few miles south of Pec, the Visoki Decani Monastery has famous wall paintings from a century later. Ecclesiastical frescoes like these, depicting scenes from the Bible and from the lives of the saints, are among the great treasures of world art. Coming across these treasures in isolated mountain settings makes them even more remarkable.

Another example of the lasting influence of the Church is in the medieval songs and chants. The Cetinje Monastery has one of Europe's oldest and largest collections of liturgical music. The pure and somewhat haunting sounds are still sung and recorded by choral groups from many parts of the world.

A LONG TRADITION IN ART

Art has a remarkably long history in all of the former Yugoslavian countries. For instance, at Lepenski Vir on the Danube River, one of Europe's most famous archaeological sites, archaeologists have found stone sculptures. These life-size statues of humans dating back to 6000 B.C. are among the oldest known sculptures.

In addition, examples of architecture from more recent history can be found throughout the country. The grandeur of the Roman Empire is visible throughout the region in the ruins of temples, amphitheaters (*below*), fortresses, and other buildings dating back some 2000 years. These relics are now carefully preserved as national artistic treasures.

MODERN ART

Modern art in Serbia and Montenegro makes use of folk motifs and often combines them with political symbols to interpret the country's chaotic recent history. Modernistic posters depict political messages, particularly outrage at the indiscriminate violence and suffering of war. In the late 1990s art groups often displayed what they called phobjects—modernistic posters plastered on the battered walls of bombed-out buildings.

Sculpture is another art form that has enjoyed continuing popularity. The most famous Yugoslav sculptor was Ivan Mestrovic (1883–1962). He created large, solid pieces that seem to emerge from the rock. He worked both with religious themes, as in his *My Mother at Prayer* and *Job*, and with patriotic subjects, such as his *Tomb of the Unknown Soldier*, located outside Belgrade.

The *Tomb of the Unknown Soldier*, a sculpture by Ivan Mestrovic, graces the top of Mount Avala, near Belgrade. Largely because of Mestrovic's works, sculptures have become popular attractions in parks and other public places in Serbia and Montenegro.

THE RETURN OF A LITERARY TREASURE

One of the great historical treasures of eastern Europe is the *Miroslav Gospel*. This is the oldest known Cyrillic document in the region. Illustrated with detailed miniatures, *The Gospel* was created in the 12th century at Saint Peter's Church in Bijelo Polje. Both Montenegrins and Serbs claim the work as their own.

The priceless volume was nearly lost during World War I, when a Serb army unit, retreating to escape the advancing Austrian army, carried it in a saddlebag through the mountains of Greece. Several years later it was returned from the island of Crete and presented to the king of Yugoslavia. It is now on display at the National Museum in Belgrade (*below*).

LITERATURE

Nationalist strivings of the Serbs and Montenegrins inspired the first great literary efforts. In 1847 Petar II Petrovic Njegos, the bishop-prince of Montenegro, wrote an epic drama called *The Mountain Wreath* (*Gorski Vijenac*) using the rhythms of folktales. Also in the 19th century, Karadzic collected examples of the South Slavic oral tradition—folk songs, poems, stories, and myths. His *Serbian Folk Poems* filled four volumes, and he also published a book of popular stories and a collection of Serbian proverbs. His collections are well-known throughout Europe, and songwriters have continued to develop new folk songs.

Although some writers produced novels in the late 1800s, it was not until the World War II novels of Ivo Andric that this form of Yugoslav literature achieved international recognition. Of Andric's novels, *The*

In the late 1980s, some Serbian songwriters created new folk songs in praise of Milosevic.

Nobel Prize-winning writer Ivo Andric sits at his desk in Belgrade in the 1960s.

Bridge on the Drina (1945) is probably the best known, and he won the Nobel Prize for Literature in 1961. His books are now regarded as classics, even though many Bosniak critics feel his writings were anti-Muslim.

Another writer who had political problems was Milovan Djilas of Montenegro. In the 1950s, while he was vice president of Yugoslavia he began writing books that criticized the Communist government—a government that he had helped to create. His nonfiction book called *The New Class* (1957) was a harsh indictment of Communism that cost him his political career. In spite of these difficulties, Djilas continued to write novels, histories, essays, and memoirs.

Two other writers who gained international fame were Dobrica Cosic and Milorad Pavic. Cosic's *A Time of Death* (1878) is a moving description of the horror of World War I. Pavic is best known for his *Dictionary of the Khazars* (1984), which was written in the form of a dictionary.

Writer and politician Milovan Djilas (1911–95) talks to Marshal Tito in 1952. Djilas served in Tito's government until his open criticism of the government resulted in his imprisonment and his breakup of relations with Tito.

MUSIC AND DANCE

Like all the arts, music and dance in Serbia and Montenegro reveal a strong folk tradition. Some of the music and dance is similar to that of neighboring Bulgaria, including the instruments used. The *gajde* (GEI-de), for example, which looks like an oversized set of bagpipes, provides a wailing background sound to many songs, including folk songs that date back more than a thousand years. Combined with flutes and fiddles, the *gajde* offers a surprising richness and variety. Traditional folk songs from different regions also accompany folk-dance groups, each group wearing costumes and following the traditional steps from their own colorful past.

There are numerous variations on the folk traditions. In Kosovo, for example, many people enjoy Turkish-style music, with instruments and tunes that originated in the Muslim Middle East. Others prefer the loud, brassy sounds of *blemuzika* (BLE-mu-zee-ka)—best exemplified by Serbia's national brass band. *Blemuzika*, which means brass music, has been heavily influenced by the brass bands of Turkey and Austria. If Serbia has a national music, this is it, and the annual festival brings dozens of brass bands together.

Some modern musicians, like Momcilo Bajagic and Djorde Balasevic, build on well-known folk themes by adding jazz rhythms and street poetry, which sound much like rap. This combination is particularly popular with young people. Two groups that have emerged since 2001 are Darkwood Dub and Eyesburn. The first combines traditional themes with rock and

Two men from eastern Serbia dressed in traditional shepherd attire, which includes a woolen cap, play the flute during a festival.

electronic music, while Eyesburn blends tradition with hard rock and a smattering of reggae.

Other types of modern music are also part of the thriving music industry. For example, a type of song known as neofolk is especially popular among rural families and industrial workers, much like country rock in the United States. Serbian rock groups are consistently popular, and many have been active in social or political movements, such as the antiwar protests of the 1990s and the anti-Milosevic movement of 1999–2002. Many Serbian musicians also express their political views through their music.

Opera, ballet, and classical orchestral music continue to have a small but dedicated following that has continued since the mid-1800s. Proximity to Vienna and Austria has influenced this popularity.

Del Arno Band, a Serbian reggae band, performs in Belgrade. The band supports the opponents of the Milosevic regime.

FILM AND THEATER

Yugoslav filmmakers produced some of the best films of the entire Communist world. This trend began in the closing months of World War II, when some experimental filmmakers began making documentaries about their war-torn land. They next turned to animated films and then to feature films. The tradition begun by these pioneers continues in the early years of the 21st century, and film remains an important medium for social and political commentary.

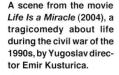

A scene from the movie *Life Is a Miracle* (2004), a tragicomedy about life during the civil war of the 1990s, by Yugoslav director Emir Kusturica.

Probably the best-known director is Emir Kusturica, a Bosnian who lives in Belgrade. He gained international fame in 1985, when his film *When Father Was Away on Business* was nominated for an Academy

Award in the Foreign Language Film category. He has also won European awards for several films, including *Time of the Gypsies, Underground* (1995) and *White Cat, Black Cat* (1997). Films dealing with war-related themes continue to impress film audiences, including *Powder Keg* (1998) by Goran Paskaljevic, and Danis Tanovic's *No Man's Land* (2001), about an encounter between two soldiers—a Serb and a Bosniak—trapped in the same trench during the civil war.

Since 1971 Belgrade has hosted a non-competitive international film festival (FEST), the only such festival held in Eastern Europe. FEST 2003 screened 95 films from 40 countries.

Theater is also a vibrant part of the country's cultural life. The National Theater in Belgrade is the center for live drama, with some plays produced in the language of Slovenia, in addition to those produced in Serbo-Croatian.

The National Theater in Belgrade stages plays and performances from all over Europe. The theater was built in 1869.

LEISURE

AFTER MORE THAN A DECADE of upheaval, the people of Serbia and Montenegro are eager to enjoy 21st-century life, but the recovery has not been a smooth one. In the past, for example, Yugoslavia was a magnet for tourists, with picturesque villages dotting the coast of the Adriatic Sea. But most of that coastline is part of Croatia, leaving Serbia and Montenegro with only 150 miles (241.4 km) of seacoast. Also, the fear of renewed unrest has made many Europeans reluctant to return.

The relocation of hundreds of thousands of refugees has also made rebuilding difficult. In 1998 and 1999 alone, more than 850,000 people fled Kosovo—both before and during the NATO bombing raids. As they return, many Serbs have to be protected from angry crowds of Kosovars. In addition, there are questions about the stability of the new political structure. Movements for independence remain strong in Montenegro and also in the provinces of Kosovo and Vojvodina.

The drive to lead normal lives remains strong, however, and the people seem energetic and determined. The downtown areas of Belgrade, Novi Sad, and other cities are once again characterized by traffic jams and sidewalks crowded with shoppers, office workers, UN officials, and vacationers. Bright lights again draw customers to shops, theaters, restaurants, and dance clubs, while the colorful umbrellas of sidewalk cafés burst open like spring blossoms whenever the sun shines.

Leisure activities range from vigorous outdoor sports, such as hunting and skiing, to quieter pastimes, such as watching movies or television and playing cards. Young people enjoy playing video games, listening to loud rock music, and prowling the new shopping malls near a few cities.

Above: **Serbs enjoy a day of shopping and browsing at market stalls in Sremska Street in Belgrade.**

Opposite: **Serbs and Montenegrins enjoy a summer day at the beach in Kotor, Montenegro. Beaches along Montenegro's Adriatic coast are popular holiday spots for both Serbs and Montenegrins and other Europeans.**

Boats moored to a pier in Kotor Bay, Montenegro, await tourists eager to enjoy a ride along Serbia and Montenegro's famous bay.

HUNTING AND FISHING

The rugged mountains and sparkling streams of Serbia and Montenegro have lured hunters and fishers from all over the Balkans and the rest of Europe for 200 years or more. Many are drawn by big game such as the Carpathian red deer, known for its large antlers; the swift and dangerous wild boar; and the big Bosnian brown bear. Many animal species that have become rare or extinct in other parts of Europe are still plentiful here. The same is true of game birds, including pheasant, grouse, and waterfowl.

Since the 1980s and the beginnings of the Green Movement, there has been a new interest in hunting with binoculars and a camera rather than a rifle or shotgun. The marsh regions of Carsks and Obedska Bara offer more than 200 species of birds in fields carpeted with marsh wildflowers.

There are 35 fishing centers in Serbia and another 10 in Montenegro. The many lakes, as well as rivers such as the Sava, Tisa, and Danube, offer an abundance of fish, including bass, carp, catfish, pike, sturgeon, trout, perch, and salmon. At a well-known fishing center on the Danube, fishers can fish and participate in the Golden Kettle of the Danube—a contest in which the competing chefs create a gigantic stew containing more than 50 types of fish.

In Durmitor National Park, 18 crystal clear lakes offer outstanding fishing, as do the region's mountain streams.

Serbian teenagers fish at the moat surrounding a medieval fortress in Smederevo, a town located along the right bank of the Danube River.

SPAS

Spas have a long tradition in Serbia. Most lie at the foot of a mountain, surrounded by forest. The mild climates, natural beauty, and therapeutic qualities of thermal mineral springs draws thousands of visitors annually. The Soko Grad spa tourist resort is located between Mounts Rtan and Ozren. This area has been a tourist destination for 150 years.

SEASONAL ACTIVITIES

Durmitor National Park is also a favorite place for weekend getaways or vacations. Camping, hiking, and mountain climbing (locally called mountaineering) are popular, as well as fishing. Hikers enjoy trekking around the lakes. Even the largest, Crno Jezero, is no more than a day's hike. And on hot summer days, walking around a lake offers hikers the chance to cool off with a refreshing swim.

Another feature of Durmitor is Tara Canyon, where the churning rapids of the Tara River offer a spectacular challenge to white-water rafters. Other swift rivers, such as the Bistrica at the Rugova Gorge and tributaries of the

Serbs enjoy a summer day playing a game of volleyball on the shores of the Danube River in Novi Sad. The bridge in the background was destroyed by a NATO bomb during the civil war.

Danube, are inviting both to rafters and to hikers. The Danube Regatta is held every summer and involves the cities of Belgrade, Novi Sad, and Smederevo.

Montenegro's coastline has many beautiful beaches. The so-called Budvan Riviera surrounds the city of Budva, the Montenegrin center of culture and tourism. Budva's old town was destroyed in a 1979 earthquake and rebuilt as a tourist attraction.

Horseback riding is also popular, and every summer the towns of Pozarevac and Lubicevo host the International Equestrian Games. Other summer sports include cycling, rock climbing, and paragliding.

Both Serbia and Montenegro and Bosnia-Herzegovina are famous for winter sports, and the Bosnian capital of Sarajevo was the site of the 1984 Olympic Games. Serbia is best known for skiing, and the 26 runs at Kopaonik bring skiers from every corner of Europe. Another famous skiing venue is Brezovica, which gives Kosovo some of the tourist trade. The same is true of Montenegro's winter resorts, such as Zabljak.

The mountains of Serbia and Montenegro are ideal for skiing in winter. The Brezovica ski resort, located in the Dinaric Alps in Kosovo, attract skiers from all over the country.

Young Serbs enjoy themselves at a party held at Zoo, a popular club in Belgrade.

ENTERTAINMENT

Serbs and Montenegrins spend a good deal of their free time with their families. The midday meal is often a festive occasion, especially on weekends and holidays, when it is likely to include family stories, games, or dancing. Some families enjoy an evening in front of the television set, but most still prefer an evening walk through their town or through one of the new malls on the outskirts of Belgrade or Novi Sad. The evening stroll is often along the walls of a citadel or on a pedestrian boulevard from which motor vehicles have been excluded, a walk that takes people past a variety of architectural styles dating back 15 or 20 centuries.

Sidewalk cafés are a popular stop for a drink, such as one of the well-known regional wines or beers, or for Turkish coffee or espresso. The nightspots feature live music, ranging from traditional folk songs to jazz, rock, and even hip-hop. Often the name of the club indicates the type of music offered, such as The Chicago Jazz Club or The Boom-Boom Room.

In Belgrade, party life is featured in a stretch of more than 20 barges and boats docked on the Danube and Sava rivers. The city has more sophisticated entertainment as well, including the National Theater, founded in the mid-1800s, and the Belgrade Philharmonia.

Several cities and towns are restoring historic areas, recreating neighborhoods centered around relaxation and enjoyment. In Belgrade, for example, Skadarska Street now has rebuilt cobblestone walkways (no motor vehicles), and features strolling musicians in folk costumes and a variety of shops and cafés.

For many, leisure activities involve simple pleasures. This is particularly true for people living in rural areas. In fact, tourists from other parts of Europe have recently become attracted to the idea of staying with a rural family, perhaps engaging in a little farmwork and then enjoying hikes through meadows blanketed with wildflowers or into the mountains.

Serbs enjoy meeting with friends in the casual and relaxed atmosphere of an outdoor café in Pec, Kosovo.

Above: **Serbia's Nenad Djordjevic (*right*) gets the ball away from England's Wayne Rooney (*left*) during a friendly soccer match between the national teams of Serbia and Montenegro, and England in June 2003 at Walkers Stadium, Leicester.**

Opposite: **Young Serbs enjoy a game of basketball at a court set up below the clock tower and fortress in Belgrade.**

SPORTS

The people of Serbia and Montenegro engage in a wide range of both individual and team sports. Soccer is immensely popular, and the original Yugoslavia fielded excellent national teams in the competition for the World Cup—the most popular sports event in the world. Amateur and professional teams are active throughout the country, and many local clubs compete in semiprofessional leagues.

Soccer is also the major spectator sport, and every city has a stadium, usually filled to capacity for matches between professional teams. The stadiums are also used for track-and-field events, and indoor auditoriums are used for events such as boxing, wrestling, weight lifting, and gymnastics.

The upheaval of the 1990s has had a lingering effect on sports in the region. From 1992 to 1996, the country was banned from most international events, including World Cup soccer. At the start of the 21st century, some teams from other countries continue to be reluctant to travel to Serbia and Montenegro out of fear of new outbreaks of violence. In the preliminary round for the World Cup, for example, Belgrade was to host the Group 9 matches for the Euro 2004 competition, but several teams asked for a change of venue in the interest of safety.

Although soccer is the most popular sport in Serbia and Montenegro, basketball is becoming more popular. It is probably the fastest-growing team sport in the country, especially among teenage boys and young men. Local teams and pickup games have popped up all over the country.

Television coverage has increased interest, and fans closely follow the careers of regional players who have made it to the U.S. National Basketball Association (NBA) or one of the European leagues.

Fencing is one of the most popular sports. It is also one of the oldest, dating back to the 1500s. Other individual sports that have small but avid followings include gymnastics, wrestling, weight lifting, cycling, ice-skating, tennis, and track-and-field events.

Serbia and Montenegro was represented by 87 athletes in 14 sports at the 2004 Olympic Games in Athens.

FESTIVALS

DURING THE DIFFICULT TIMES of the 1990s, the festive spirit seemed to disappear from Yugoslav life, but that spirit has enjoyed a great resurgence at the start of the 21st century. Both religious and secular celebrations are again popular, with many festivals of both kinds taking place over the course of the year. The difference in religions creates variety, and even when two religions observe the same holiday, their festivals may be very different, and even held at different times. For example, Roman Catholics and Protestants celebrate Christmas on December 25, but the Eastern Orthodox Church celebrates it on January 7.

Secular festivals are also varied, with each city or region hosting its own events. The most popular celebrations are those associated with the arts. In fact, from May to November there is always a festival of music, art, theater, or film somewhere in Serbia and Montenegro.

Left: **A Serb Orthodox Christian kisses an icon placed at the entrance of a church during Easter. Orthodox Christians kiss icons depicting Jesus Christ, the saints, and scenes from the Bible, to show humility and devotion toward the people depicted in the icons.**

Opposite: **A Serbian man carries a wooden cross decorated with flowers through the streets of Belgrade during a Serbian Orthodox procession on Patron Saint's Day.**

FESTIVALS FOR THE ARTS

The city of Belgrade leads the parade of annual events dedicated to the arts, beginning with the annual film festival—FEST—in February. FEST draws moviemakers, critics, actors, and film buffs from all over Europe and the Middle East. By May the city is in its full festival mode, with celebrations that include Belgrade Spring—a celebration of song with open-air performances by individuals and groups.

This is followed in June by the International Festival of Children's Folk Songs and Dances, which was suspended through most of the 1990s, but now appears to be fully restored. The Summer Jazz Festival is a continuous celebration from June to September. In September, Belgrade hosts the International Theater Festival, followed in October by a festival of classical music and a monthlong art show called The October Salon.

Serbian girls dress up in traditional costume for a festival. Serbian traditional costumes for girls include a heavily-embroidered robe with sleeves and a red cap, for single girls, or headscarf, for married women.

The country's second largest city, Novi Sad, also offers a series of colorful celebrations. In May, Novi Sad hosts the Sterijino Pozorje Drama Festival and, in the same month, the Jovan Jovanovic Zmaj Children's Poetry Festival. In August, bands come from all over Europe for what is called the Exit Music Festival held in the Petrovaradin Citadel.

Several other cities also hold festivals in their historic fortresses. Budva has a summer music festival in its citadel, and in Nis, the summerlong Festival of Jazz and Blues is held in that city's fortress.

One of the loudest and most popular events is the Festival of Brass Bands at Guca, a town near Cacak, in August. Brass bands from all over Europe join in a noisy and joyful battle of bands. Other popular festivals include the Suncane Skale Music Festival held in July at Herceg-Novi on Kotor Bay. In this Mediterranean setting, people enjoy open-air theatrical performances as well as concerts.

Serbian actors in a play staged at the Atelje 212 Theater in Belgrade. The theater, which originally had 212 seats, was founded in 1956 and soon became the showcase for the new avant-garde drama that was popular in Europe at the time. In 1967 the theater hosted the first BITEF (Belgrade International Theater Festival), an annual avant-garde theater event.

EASTERN ORTHODOX HOLIDAYS

The Serbian Orthodox Church follows the Julian calendar that was established by Julius Caesar in 45 B.C. In the 20th century other Eastern Orthodox churches followed the practice of the Roman Catholic and Protestant churches in their use of the Gregorian calendar. The Julian calendar can place Easter anywhere from one to five weeks later than the Catholic and Protestant Easter.

In Eastern Orthodox communities, each family fills a basket with traditional Easter foods—a festive cake, dyed eggs, cheese, and butter

Patriarch Pavle, the head of the Serbian Orthodox Church, leads priests through the church, during an Easter service in Belgrade.

(often in the shape of a lamb). On Easter Sunday (or Monday in some communities), they take this basket to the church where the items are placed on a long table with the goods of all the other families. The people sing as the priest walks around the table blessing all the foods.

Serbian Christmas is celebrated on January 7. On Christmas Eve a Yule log is placed on the fire as family and friends enjoy a large meal that might end with a Christmas cake containing a coin. Whoever receives the piece of cake with the coin is supposed to have good luck in the coming year. Three weeks prior to Christmas, *Detinjci* (de-TEEN-tsi), or Day of the Child, is observed. The following Sunday is Mother's Day and the third Sunday honors fathers. These three days emphasize close family ties.

During an Easter service, Serbian Orthodox Christians line up to receive a cup containing water from the miraculous fountain in St. Petka Chapel in Belgrade.

A priest blesses the cake at the celebration of the Ascension of our Lord, the patron saint's day of Visoki Decani Monastery in Kosovo.

PATRON SAINT'S DAY

Each Serbian family celebrates their Patron Saint's Day—Slava or Krsna Slava—a day that has been set aside to honor the family's saint or protector. The same saint is honored from generation to generation, passed down from father to son. This tradition began before the arrival of Christianity, when families worshiped individual gods. Once converted to Christianity, the Serbs transferred this observance to the Christian saints. Families sometimes chose a particular saint because the saint's celebration day was near to the day of the family's conversion to Christianity.

The Krsna Slava ritual involves a series of symbols— a candle, wheat, and bread. Customs vary from region to region, but everywhere the basic idea is the same: the day is spent worshiping the patron saint by offering a bloodless sacrifice. Traditionally, the family attends church, taking with them a *Slavski Kolac* (SLAH-vskee KOH-lahk), or Patron Saint's Cake; a bowl of cooked wheat sweetened with honey or sugar called *koljivo* (kohl-YEE-voh); and a memorial book that lists the family's deceased relatives. The priest cuts and blesses the Patron Saint's Cake.

At home the cake and wheat dish are placed on the table along with a candle, which is left to burn all day. Relatives and friends are invited to join in a celebration dinner. The host (always the male head of the household) prays to God and his patron saint and then serves his guests. Every guest receives a small portion of the cake and the wheat dish.

THE ISLAMIC MONTH OF RAMADAN

For Muslims, the most important period is the month of Ramadan—the ninth month in Islam's lunar calendar. Throughout the month the faithful pray and observe a strict fast every day from sunrise to sunset. Following Ramadan, the first three days in the month of Shawwal are devoted to a great festival called Id-al-Fitr, the Feast of the Fast Breaking. People gather with family and friends for three days of feasting, congregational prayers, and the exchanging of gifts. In some cities and towns, street fairs are held, featuring music and kiosks offering food for sale; minarets are decorated with strings of little white lights.

Ethnic Albanian Muslim men leave a mosque in Presevo, Serbia, after prayers.

FOOD

THE FOODS OF SERBIA AND MONTENEGRO are something like a great international smorsgasbord, with popular dishes influenced by the cuisines of Turkey, Greece, Italy, Hungary, Germany, and several other countries. No matter the country of origin, every favored recipe seems to include meat in some form—roasts, steaks, grilled strips, ground meat, kebabs, sausages, and so on. Even breakfast usually includes meat, such as the popular *burek* (BU-rek)—a rather heavy pie containing layers of cheese and ground meat.

Fast foods are available everywhere, at street kiosks as well as cafés and restaurants. The most popular fast food is *cevapcici* (ce-VAP-chee-chee)—spicy sausage served on hearty pita bread. *Burek* is also served as a fast food.

Left: **A Montenegrin man prepares a hamburger. Grilled meats are a favorite throughout the region.**

Opposite: **Typical dishes from Montenegro feature fresh fish and seafood, caught from the nearby Adriatic coast.**

REGIONAL VARIATIONS

Restaurants throughout the country offer a wide variety of foods, and each region also has certain specialties. In Vojvodina, for example, the cuisine in people's homes as well as in restaurants shows a strong Hungarian influence. Many recipes call for generous portions of paprika, and Hungarian goulash comes close to being a national dish. Another spicy Vojvodina favorite is called *alaska corba* (ah-LAHS-ka CHORE-ba), which is described as a fiery river-fish stew.

SERBIAN DISHES

The foods of Serbia are famous in their own right, especially for grilled meat, including *cevapcici* and *pljeskavica* (PLYES-ka-vee-tsa) —something like a large hamburger, but very spicy (this, too, is a popular fast food). Another well-known grilled dish is the Serbian version of shish kebab called *raznjici* (razh-NJEE-chee)—made with chunks of veal or pork on a skewer with onions and peppers. A hearty combination platter of *cevapcici*, *pljeskavica*, and *raznjici* is a popular menu item in restaurants; it is called *mesano mes* (MEH-sha-no MEH-so), or mixed grill. Another typical Serbian dish is *duvec* (JEW-vech)—grilled pork cutlets

PAPRIKA

Outdoor markets throughout Serbia and Montenegro sell many varieties of paprika. Paprika seasoning ranges from mild to the very hot. The fruit of *Capsium annuum linne* plants are sold fresh or dried, and eaten raw or cooked, pickled, or milled into paprika. Each of these forms is featured in Yugoslav cuisine. Bell peppers and tomato paprika are used to make stuffing of rice (*right*), meat, or cheese. A bit of yogurt or sour cream may be served to take away the heat of the paprika.

Both green and ripe red varieties can be roasted, peeled, and served whole seasoned with oil, vinegar, and chopped garlic. The hottest varieties, mixed with chopped onion, sometimes accompany grilled meats. Hot and spicy foods are common in Serbia and Montenegro.

mixed with spiced stewed peppers, zucchini, and tomatoes and served over rice. Just about all of these foods are heavily spiced. Even Serbian salad is anything but subtle—raw peppers with sliced onions and tomatoes and a dressing of oil and vinegar.

MONTENEGRIN DISHES

Regional recipes from Montenegro often include dairy products, such as a favorite called *kajmak* (KAJ-mak), made with cream, which is then salted and allowed to harden. The Greek influence is evident in *musaka* (MU-sa-ka)—eggplant and potatoes placed in alternating layers with ground meat (either lamb or beef). Recipes with a Turkish or Middle Eastern touch include shish kebab and *kapama* (kah-PAH-mah), stewed lamb mixed with spinach, onions, and yogurt. The Middle Eastern influence is also found in *sarma* (SAR-ma) (stuffed cabbage rolls) and *punjena tikvica* (PUN-je-na TEEK-vee-tsa) (stuffed zucchini); in both dishes the filling is ground beef or lamb and rice.

Opposite: **A young Serbian girl dressed in traditional costume carries a tray with typical Serbian salted bread during a village festival.**

A rural couple in Montenegro show off home-made plum brandy, which they have distilled in their farm.

FRUIT AND DESSERTS

In most families desserts are light—a simple cake or pudding and whatever fruits are available, with plums being an unofficial national fruit. Apples, grapes, melons, pomegranates, and pears are also popular. On special occasions a family will have *baklava* (bak-LA-va), an import from Turkey, or Viennese-style tortes.

The fruits of Serbia and Montenegro are also used to make the favorite wines and brandies. Serbian and Montenegrin wines are highly regarded and are sold worldwide. In Serbia, the most popular drink is a plum brandy called *sljivovica* (SHLYEE-vo-vee-tsa), but Montenegrins prefer a potent grape brandy.

RECIPES YUGOSLAV-STYLE

Preparing meals can be a long, labor-intensive process, especially in rural areas, where precooked and packaged foods have not yet become popular.

For example, to make a heavy cream called *kajmak*, milk is boiled in a shallow enamel pan. Next, a pint of heavy cream is poured in from as great a height as the cook can manage. The milk-and-cream combination is then simmered for about two hours; the cook turns off the heat, and the mixture is allowed to stand for six hours.

After the six hours, the stove is turned on again and the mixture simmers for another half hour. Once the pan is cooled, it is placed in the refrigerator for 24 hours. The cream is now complete. The *kajmak* is loosened with a knife, placed on a plate, and cut into squares. It can be served as is, or it can be used in place of whipped cream.

Even coffee preparation can become quite involved. Special, often beautifully decorated equipment is used for roasting, grinding, brewing, and serving *Turska kafa* (TUR-ska ka-FA), or Turkish coffee.

TURSKA KAFA (TURKISH COFFEE)

4 heaping teaspoons instant coffee
   (Turkish coffee if available)
3 heaping teaspoons sugar
$1^{1}/_{2}$ cups water

Bring the water to a boil in a small saucepan (or a Turkish coffeepot). While the water is heating, put coffee, sugar, and 1 tablespoon water in a cup, and stir it until smooth and blended. When the water boils, pour in the coffee mixture and bring it to a boil again. Turn off the heat, let the coffee settle, and serve immediately.

Serbian and Montenegrin women buy fresh vegetables and produce at the central covered market in Belgrade.

SHOPPING

In most of the country, people shop every day or two. Supermarkets are now available in or near Belgrade and a few other cities, but most people prefer to shop at open-air markets, where they can select fruit and vegetables from open bins and crates.

Meats, with lamb and beef being the most popular, are purchased from a butcher's stall where shoppers choose cuts and amounts that are not prepackaged.

MEALTIMES

Since most people begin work between 6 and 8 A.M., breakfast is an early, hearty meal. Tea, milk, or strong coffee is served with pastries or bread and meat or eggs, or both. For most families the main meal of the day is served around 2 P.M., and many workers come home for a long dinner hour, and then work until 7 or 8 P.M. The meal usually begins with a thick homemade soup, followed by the main meat dish, then salad and dessert. Supper is generally a light meal and is served around 8 P.M.

Beverages are generally served after the main course. Adults drink bottled water, coffee, or beer, while children have milk, occasionally a soft drink, or a thin yogurt-based drink called *kefir* (KE-feer).

An ethnic Albanian family in Kosovo partakes a meal of cheese and bread.

SLATKO (SWEET JAM)

Serbian families often welcome visitors with a cup of thick jam called *slatko* ("SLAT-ko"), whether they are coming for just a visit, for tea, or plan to stay for dinner.

4 plums or 2 peaches
2 cups sugar
$^1/_2$ cup water
2 teaspoons lemon juice

Wash the fruit, remove the pits, and cut it into small cubes. Place sugar and water in a saucepan, bring it to a boil, and continue boiling over a low heat until the mixture thickens. Add the fruit and cook only long enough for it to be cooked through, about 20 minutes. Add the lemon juice, mix, and pour it into a clean jar.

Note: If the slatko is to be stored, like jam, then the jar must be sterile and sealed properly; this recipe is for use within a few days. Refrigerate the slatko until chilled or overnight. When guests first arrive, give each person a half-cup serving in a cup or small bowl, with a teaspoon and a glass of water.

SALATA OD VRUCHEG KROMPIRA

This recipe for warm potato salad, or *salata od vrucheg krompira* (sa-LAH-ta ot VRU-cheg krom-PEE-rah), makes 4 to 6 servings.

6 medium potatoes
1 tablespoon butter
1 cup finely chopped celery
2 tablespoons chopped parsley
1 chopped onion
4 tablespoons salad oil or olive oil
4 tablespoons vinegar
1 teaspoon salt
$^1/_2$ teaspoon pepper
$^1/_2$ teaspoon paprika

Boil the potatoes whole until done, but firm. Let cool, then peel and slice very thin. Use the butter to coat a baking dish, and place the potato slices in it. Sprinkle the celery, parsley, and onion over the potato slices as evenly as possible. Mix the oil, vinegar, salt, pepper, and paprika together. Pour this dressing evenly over the potato mixture. Cover the baking dish, and heat in the oven for about 15 minutes. Serve warm.

A B C D

1

CROATIA

Subotica

V O J V O D I N A

P a n n o n i a n   P l a i n

Drava

Danube

Tisa

Novi Sad
Beocin
Petrovaradin

Sremska
Mitrovica

Sava

2

BELGRADE

Mount
Avala ▲

● Pancevo

Smederevo   ● Pozarevac

Danube

ROMANIA

Sip ✕ Iron Gate
● Djerdap

BOSNIA-
HERZEGOVINA

S E R B I A

Bor ●

3

● Kragujevac

● Cacak
Guca ● Kraljevo ● ● Rekovac

Soko Banja ●

Ibar

Kapaonik   Mountains

● Kapaonik

Nis ●

Balkan   Mountains

D i n a r i c

Black Lake
Zabljak ●

Tara

▲ Mount Durmitor
(8,275 ft / 2,522 m)

4

Niksic ●

A l p s

MONTENEGRO

Brezovica ●

● Mededi
Potok

● Pec

BULGARIA

Gracanica ● ● Pristina

K O S O V O

CROATIA

Kotor ● Podgorica ●
● Cetinje

Herceg-Novi

Gulf of Kotor

Sveti
Stefan ●

▲ Mount Daravica
(8,712 ft / 2,656 m)

Vitina ●

● Presevo

Budva ●

*Lake
Scutari*

Prizren ●

Sharr   Mountains

Stari Bar ●
● Bar

5

A D R I A T I C

S E A

ALBANIA

MACEDONIA

N

International boundary
Republic boundary
Autonomous boundary
● Capital city

Feet   Meters
9,900   3,000
6,600   2,000
3,300   1,000
1,650   500
660   200
0   0

MAP OF SERBIA AND MONTENEGRO

ECONOMIC SERBIA AND MONTENEGRO

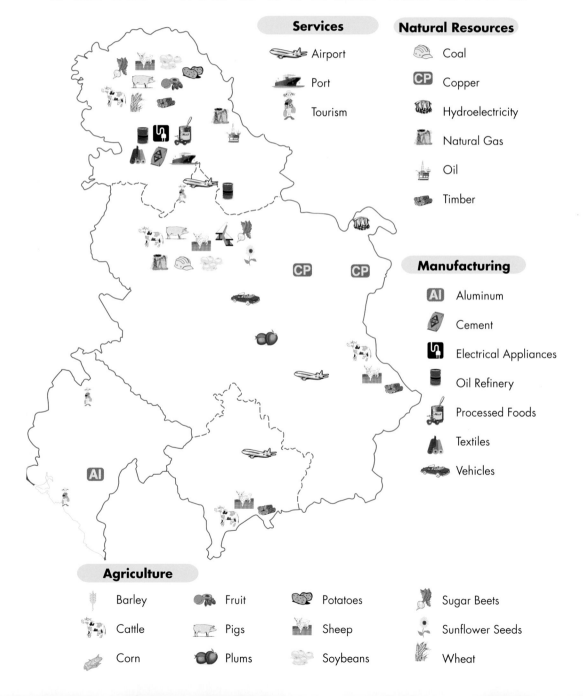

Services
- Airport
- Port
- Tourism

Natural Resources
- Coal
- CP Copper
- Hydroelectricity
- Natural Gas
- Oil
- Timber

Manufacturing
- AI Aluminum
- Cement
- Electrical Appliances
- Oil Refinery
- Processed Foods
- Textiles
- Vehicles

Agriculture
- Barley
- Cattle
- Corn
- Fruit
- Pigs
- Plums
- Potatoes
- Sheep
- Soybeans
- Sugar Beets
- Sunflower Seeds
- Wheat

ABOUT THE ECONOMY

GDP
US$23.15 billion (2002)

PER CAPITA GDP
US$2,200 (2002)

GDP SECTORS
Agriculture 2.3 percent; mining and manufacturing 18.5 percent; construction, public utilities, transportation, communication, and trade 25.7 percent; public administration and defense 13.7 percent; other (including 1 million unemployed) 41.8 percent (2000)

LAND AREA
39,450 square miles (102,175 square km)

FORESTED LAND
35 percent

UNEMPLOYMENT RATE
30 percent (2002 estimate)

CURRENCY
Serbia: Serbian dinar (CSD) (*below left*)
1 dinar = 100 paras
USD 1 = CSD 67.30
Montenegro: Euro (EUR) (*below right*)
USD 1 = EUR 0.84

AGRICULTURAL PRODUCTS
Fruit, grains, vegetables; cattle, goats, pigs, poultry, sheep

MINERALS
Antimony, bauxite, coal, chrome, copper, gas, gold, lead, nickel, oil, pyrite, zinc

INDUSTRIES
Chemicals, consumer goods, electronics, machinery, mining, petroleum products, pharmaceuticals, steel

MAJOR EXPORTS
Chemicals, machinery, petroleum products, pharmaceuticals

MAJOR IMPORTS
Electronic equipment, food, motor vehicles

MAJOR TRADING PARTNERS
Bosnia-Herzegovina, Italy, Macedonia

PORTS AND HARBORS
Bar, Novi Sad

INFLATION RATE
10 percent (2003)

POVERTY RATE
30 percent

LEADING FOREIGN INVESTORS
European Union (EU), United States

CULTURAL SERBIA AND MONTENEGRO

Gallery of Frescoes
Displays reproductions of the famous frescoes found in churches and monasteries throughout the former Yugoslavia.

Kalemegdan Citadel
Built in the fourth century A.D. the fortress is one of the country's most famous landmarks.

Petrovaradin Citadel
Built in the 1700s, the citadel was known as the Gibraltar of the Danube, now a favorite place for evening strolls.

Skadarska Street
A restored area of Old Town, with cobblestone streets, shops, and cafés.

National Theater
Built in the 1860s, the theater is one of the most famous in the Balkans.

Sremska Mitrovica
Built on the ruins of the ancient Roman city of Sirmium—birthplace of five Roman emperors.

Durmitor National Park
A beautiful resort area with 18 mountain lakes, popular for hiking, swimming, fishing, and other outdoor activities.

Danube River
The famous Iron Gate canal squeezes the Danube River through the largest canyon in Europe.

Tara Canyon
Second only to the Grand Canyon for its depth and length.

Kalenic Monastery (near Rekovac)
Known as the rainbow monastery for its many colors.

Zabljak
A picturesque ski resort and the highest town in Serbia and Montenegro.

Gadime Cave
Famous for its helictites (stalactites that grow at strange angles).

Lake Scutari
Yugoslavia's largest lake. A popular tourist attraction known for excellent fishing.

Kosovo Palin
Site of the historic 14th-century battle in which the Ottoman Turks defeated the Serbian army. The subject of many folktales, songs, and poems.

ABOUT THE CULTURE

OFFICIAL NAME
Serbia and Montenegro

NATIONAL FLAG
Three horizontal bars, with blue on top, white in the center, red across the bottom. From 1945 to the mid-1990s, a large red star in the center stood for Communism.

NATIONAL ANTHEM
Hej Saveni (*Hey Slavs*) was the Yugoslavian national anthem with lyrics in Serbo-Croatian, Slovenian, and Macedonian. Today it is sung in Serbian with lyrics by Samuel Tomasik.

CAPITAL
Belgrade

OTHER MAJOR CITIES
Kragujevac, Novi Sad, Nis, Podgorica

POPULATION
Serbia 5,763,000; Montenegro 648,000; Vojvodina 2,000,000; Kosovo 2,250,000; Total 10,655,774 (2003)

POPULATION DENSITY
270.7 per square mile (104.5 per square km)

ETHNIC GROUPS
Serb 62.6 percent; Albanian 16.5 percent; Montenegrin 5.0 percent; multiethnic 3.4 percent; Hungarian 3.3 percent; Bosniak 3.2 percent; Gypsy 1.4 percent

LIFE EXPECTANCY
Male 71 years; Female 77 years

TIME
Greenwich Mean Time plus 1 hour

RELIGIOUS GROUPS
Eastern Orthodox 65 percent; Muslim 19 percent; Roman Catholic 4 percent; other (mostly nonreligious) 12 percent

OFFICIAL LANGUAGE
Serbian (also called Serbo-Croatian); Hungarian (in some regions)

EDUCATION
Free and compulsory, ages 7 to 14

LITERACY RATE
Male 98 percent; Female 89 percent

NATIONAL HOLIDAYS
Constitution Day Federation of Yugoslavia (April 27) (March 28 for Serbia); Victory Day (May 9); Flag Day (November 28) (Kosovo only)

FAMOUS SERBS
Ivo Andric (1892–1975)—Nobel prize winning author
Emir Kusturica (1954–)—film director

TIME LINE

IN SERBIA AND MONTENEGRO	IN THE WORLD
1000 B.C. Illyrians spread throughout the Balkan Peninsula.	
	753 B.C. Rome is founded.
228 B.C. Romans gain control, establish Province of Illyricum.	
	116–17 B.C. The Roman Empire reaches its greatest extent, under Emperor Trajan (98–17).
A.D. 300s Barbarian groups invade the Balkans.	
A.D. 600 Slavic tribes migrate into Balkans. South Slavs dominate area of future Yugoslavia	**A.D. 600** Height of Mayan civilization
700–900 Entire region becomes part of the Byzantine Empire; Saint Cyril and Saint Methodius spread Orthodox Christianity.	**1000** The Chinese perfect gunpowder and begin to use it in warfare.
1168 Stefan Nemansa rules the land that becomes Serbia.	
1331–35 Serbia's "Golden Age" under Stephen Dusan	
1389 Ottoman Turks defeat the Serbs in the Battle of Kosovo.	**1776** U.S. Declaration of Independence
	1789–99 The French Revolution
1804–15 Serb uprisings against Turkish rule.	
1830 Independence of Serbia recognized by the great powers of Europe.	**1861** The U.S. Civil War begins.
1867 Last Turkish forces evacuate Serbia.	
1878 Turkey and Europe recognize the independence of Serbia and Montenegro.	
1912–13 Balkan Wars	**1914** World War I begins.

IN SERBIA AND MONTENEGRO	IN THE WORLD
1919 Treaty of Versailles recognizes the Kingdom of Serbs, Croatians, and Slovenes.	
1929 King Alexander changes the kingdom's name to Yugoslavia and establishes one-man rule.	
1934 Croatian terrorists assassinate Alexander.	**1939** World War II begins.
1941 Yugoslavia becomes ally of Axis powers; the army revolts and Germany invades; Tito leads Partisan freedom fighters.	
1944 Partisans and Russians drive out the last German divisions.	
1945 Marshal Tito becomes head of state; a Communist government is established.	**1945** The United States drops atomic bombs on Hiroshima and Nagasaki.
	1949 The North Atlantic Treaty Organization (NATO) is formed.
1980 Death of Tito.	
1991 Croatia and Slovenia declare independence from Yugoslavia; civil war erupts.	**1991** Break-up of the Soviet Union
1992 Bosnia-Herzegovina declares independence.	
1995 Serbs massacre an estimated 7,000 Bosniaks at Srebrenica; NATO air strikes against Serb positions force Serbs to sign Dayton Agreement.	**1997** Hong Kong is returned to China.
1998–99 NATO forces force Yugoslavia to agree to peace in Kosovo.	
2000–01 Slobodan Milosevic arrested and extradited to the Netherlands and War Crimes Tribunal.	**2001** Terrorists crash planes in New York, Washington, D.C., and Pennsylvania.
	2003 War in Iraq

GLOSSARY

avant-garde
Artistic group that experiments with new techniques.

Balkans
The countries occupying the Balkan peninsula.

blemuzika (BLE-mu-zee-ka)
The brass music played by Serbia's national band and other bands.

bora
An icy wind that sweeps down from the north, bringing little snow but bitter cold.

Bosniaks
Bosnians who are Muslims.

cevapcici (ce-VAP-chee-chee)
A popular Yugoslav fast food—a sausage stuffed with ground meat and spices.

ethnic cleansing
A process in which one ethnic group expels, imprisons, or kills civilians of another, usually minority, ethnic group.

frescoes
Famous wall paintings on the walls of Orthodox churches and monasteries scattered throughout Yugoslavia. Painted from the 11th to 14th century, they are among the world's greatest art treasures.

gajde (GEI-de)
Musical instrument that looks like a set of bagpipes.

Id-al-Fitr
Feast of the Fast Breaking ending the fast of Ramadan, celebrated during the first three days of Shawwal, tenth month in the Muslim calendar.

Iron Gate
A famous narrow channel in the Danube River.

karst terrain
Areas of limestone where water has eroded softer limestone creating depressions and many caves.

kula (KU-la) **houses**
A corner house in some Kosovo villages, which, for protection, has no windows on the ground floor.

kumstvo (KUM-stvo)
A form of family patronage.

Partisans
Yugoslav freedom fighters against Germany in World War II, led by Marshal Tito.

seminomadic
Describes the lifestyle in which people move to temporary dwellings during certain seasons.

tanyaks (TUN-yucks)
Scattered homesteads in Vojvodina originally built as harvest shelters.

zupan (ZHU-pun)
Serb clan leaders who sometimes gained control of large kingdoms, including Serbia itself.

FURTHER INFORMATION

BOOKS

Andryszewski, Tricia. *Kosovo: The Splintering of Yugoslavia*. Minneapolis: Millbrook Press, 2000.

Bennett, Christopher. *Yugoslavia's Bloody Collapse*. New York: NYU Press, 1995.

Collin, Matthew. *Guerrilla Radio: Rock and Roll Radio and Serbia's Underground*. New York: Nation Books, 2002.

Filipovic, Zlata. *Zlata's Diary: A Child's Life in Sarajevo*. New York: Penguin, 1997.

Harris, Nathaniel. *The War in Former Yugoslavia*. Chicago: Heinemann-Raintree, 1998.

Hupchick, Dennis P. and Harold E. Cox. *A Concise Historical Atlas of Eastern Europe*. New York: Palgrave MacMillan, 1996.

Labon, Joanna, ed. *Balkan Blues: Writing Out of Yugoslavia*. Chicago: Northwestern University Press, 1995.

Silber, Laura and Alan Little. *Yugoslavia: Death of a Nation*. New York: Penguin, 1996.

West, Rebecca. *Black Lamb, Grey Falcon: A Journey Through Yugoslavia*. New York: Viking Press, 1941.

WEBSITES

BBC Country profiles. news.bbc.co.uk/i/hi/world/Europe/country_profiles

CIA World Factbook. www.cia.gov/cia/publications/factbook/geos/yi.html

City of Belgrade. www.beograd.org.yu

The European Forum. www.europeanforum.net

Library of Congress Country Study. lcweb2.loc.gov/frdlcs/yutoc.html

Lonely Planet World Guide. www.lonelyplanet.com/destinations

Montenegro Tourism. www.visit-montenegro.com

Serbia Info. www.serbia-info.com

Serbian Unity Congress. www.suc.org/culture/

MUSIC

Anthology of Serbian Folk Music. VDE-Gallo Records, 2000.

Gypsy King of Serbia by Saban Bajramovic. Arc Music, 2003.

The Rough Guide to the Music of the Balkans. World Music Network, 2003.

VIDEO

My Country: Serbia, a documentary by Goran Radovanovic. Library Video Company, 1999.

Turmoil in Twentieth Century Europe. Discovery Channel, 2004.

Twentieth Century with Mike Wallace: Death in Yugoslavia. A&E Home Video, 1999.

BIBLIOGRAPHY

Editors of Grolier. *Lands and People.* Vol. 4, *Yugoslavia.* Danbury, CT: Grolier Publishing Co., 1993.

Editors of Lonely Planet Publications. *Eastern Europe.* Victoria, Australia: Lonely Planet Publications, 2003.

Editors of World Book. *World Book Encyclopedia of People and Places.* Vol. 6. Chicago: World Book, Inc., 2000.

Halpern, Joel and Barbara Kerewsky Halpern. *A Serbian Village in Historical Perspective.* New York: Viking Press, 1986.

MSN Website. *Learning and Research: Serbia and Montenegro.* Microsoft Corp., 2003.

Online Language Resources Website. http://onlinelearning.lingnet.org/Serbian-Croatian/Survival_Guide/default.htm

INDEX